No Pat on the Back

Confessions of a Football Pundit

Pat Spillane
as told to John Scally

BLACKWATER PRESS

Editor
Sinéad Lawton

Design & Layout
Paula Byrne

Cover Design
Melanie Gradtke

ISBN
1-84131-670-9

Produced in Ireland by
Blackwater Press
c/o Folens Publishers
Hibernian Industrial Estate
Tallaght
Dublin 24

Contents

Acknowledgements

I am very grateful to the many people who have corresponded with me either by email or letter with their stories. Particular thanks to Martin Murphy, Padraic Neary, Aidan Phelan and Terry Rehill.

Special thanks to Charles Bobbett for his technical assistance and expertise and to the great Mick Galwey for his advice.

Thanks to John O'Connor, Sinéad Lawton and all at Blackwater Press for their enthusiastic support of this book and to Catherine Tiernan and O2 for their sponsorship.

Foreword

I had the ultimate ball during my playing career. Even through the lows of my setbacks, defeats and injuries I thoroughly enjoyed myself. Even in 1982! Yet when I look around at the game that has dominated my life often I do not like what I see.

We in the GAA seem to have forgotten the origins of sport. We have lost sight of the fact that it is only a hobby, a leisure time activity. We have lost the sheer joy of Gaelic football. It should be about playing and having the craic. What it has become, though, is more like a military exercise where a battle has to be won. I am not just talking about the physical aspect, but the fact that we are importing a lot of the excesses of professional sport into our game. All the training and all the video analysis that are becoming part and parcel of the modern game are taking away from its beauty and grace. Winning is everything and whatever has to be done to win will be done. This culture has infected all levels of our game. At club level now, even if clubs want to win the most Mickey Mouse junior title, they will approach it with the zeal of an army going into battle. We are no longer catering for the social side of the game.

I think it is time to call 'Stop'. Believe me, I have no delusions about being the Messiah, but I am going to try and do my bit for the restoration of the true spirit of Gaelic football. This is something very simple: a game people play and watch and talk about for the sheer joy of doing so.

I hope this book will make a modest contribution to putting the fun back into the game I love so well. It makes no claim to literary greatness, but I hope this sideways look at the world of Gaelic football will raise a few smiles and hopefully the odd chuckle.

I am grateful to my colleagues in RTÉ Sport who have given me a second career as a pundit, especially to Niall Cogley, who gave me a new challenge as a presenter of *The Sunday Game*, to Glen Killane, who is the new head of sport in RTÉ, and to Paul Byrnes for the loyalty, help and support they have given me in recent years.

I have so much to thank the *Sunday World* for since I joined their team in 1991. In that time there has never been a cross word between us. They are an absolute joy to work for, and I have become good friends with great people like Michael Brophy, the Managing Director. Colm McGinty, the best editor in the business, is a very good friend, although my wife does not allow me to go on many social outings with him in Terenure because I always return the worse for wear! The sports editor, Brian Farrell, has been a great help and support to me, as has Seán McGoldrick who patiently listens to my outbursts every week and who did a very good job on my first book.

Templenoe GAA club has been a huge part of my life from my earliest days, and all its members provide me with an ongoing source of inspiration.

I am forever grateful to my mother, Maura, my brothers, Mick and Tom, and my sister, Margaret, who have always been there for me through good times and bad.

Finally, but most importantly, I must put on record my profound gratitude to my wife Rosarii, daughters, Cara and Shóna, and son Pat Jr., who play second fiddle to the GAA for every single weekend of the Championship as I forsake them for RTÉ. Above all, I am grateful to them for being a constant reminder to me that there is a far more rewarding and fulfilling life outside football.

Pat Spillane,
November 2004

Introduction

I still recall the moment I decided I hated Pat Spillane.

In my defence I was young at the time. I was also wired and emotional. Shortly beforehand I had experienced the best 11 minutes of my life, standing in the Canal End at Croke Park. My native Roscommon had got off to a whirlwind start and were leading the greatest team of all time by 1–2 to no score during the 1980 All-Ireland final.

Then Roscommon's momentum was halted by a controversial incident. Pat Spillane lay writhing in apparent agony on the ground. Twelve years later, I saw the video for the first time and my suspicions were confirmed. 'Is Pat Spillane really hurt or is he in line for an Oscar?' So Micheál O'Hehir wondered aloud as Gerry Fitzmaurice and Spillane were involved in an incident off the ball. Afterwards Pat was prostrate on the ground and took an age to get up. Time went by and many efforts were made to assist his recovery, to no avail. About four minutes later Pat staggered up. It did not escape my attention that Roscommon were playing with a strong wind at the time. Within a minute Pat was flying up the wing like a March hare.

A Roscommon fan standing behind me in the Canal End was so miffed by this bit of gamesmanhip that he remarked, 'There's no doubt – the two worst things about Pat Spillane is his face.'

I knew in my gut that Roscommon's All-Ireland was lost. In my eyes, Spillane became evil incarnate. Each time he tormented the Roscommon defence I whispered the two lines I could remember from a poem by Michael Hartnett which cursed a cat thief.

May your drunken uncle lose his dole.
May your only daughter get up the pole.

As the years passed, my admiration for Spillane the player grew and grew, because in full flight he caused more problems than a trapeze artist with loose bowels. Once he retired, though, all my ill-feeling returned. As a pundit he became even more famous, or infamous, than he had been as a player. This lion in winter regularly ridiculed teams from Connacht and became our greatest enemy all over again. For most of the 1990s, it would have been easier to get a Connacht football fan to knit with sawdust than to pay a compliment to Pat Spillane as he appeared to offer a worm's eye view of football in the West.

Fast forward to August 2002. By an accident of history I found myself in Pat's company for an afternoon. Within a few minutes all my deep prejudices were dissipated. By that evening I would have walked over hot coals for him. His waspish wit makes him both infuriating and cherishable. His great passion makes some, though not all, of his sins forgivable. Mind you, there are still times watching him when I have the urge to change just one thing. The channel.

Working with Pat has been an education. I never know what unique insights into Gaelic games I might find in my conversations with him. To call him controversial would be to call the Atlantic Ocean wet. He may not be sugar, but he adds plenty of spice.

Every rose has its thorns though. My biggest problem was to dissuade him from forsaking his career as a pundit because he wanted to become a screen-writer. He was so taken by the success of God's *Lethal Weapon*, Mel Gibson, earlier this year with *The Passion of the Christ,* that he wanted to write a new film in Aramaic for Christmas, based on the Nativity story. He was going to call it *There's Something About Mary.*

The other problem I encountered was that as the Championship unfolded, Pat was getting more and more angry due to his frustration with forwards who, when they got in front of goal, were like terrified virgins running away from Don Juan, with selectors without the brains to chew gum and walk in a straight line at the same time, and with managers using purely defensive tactics to name just a few. At any hint of what has now entered the vernacular as 'puke' football, his face started to go a dangerous shade of red. Fearing for his health I sent him to an anger management course for two weeks. Pat, the man you cannot gag, was sent home after just the second day. He kept getting angry with the teachers.

Pat assured me from the outset that he would not patronise me when talking about Connacht football. He promptly explained that to patronise is to talk down to someone. By and large I took his comments about football in the West pretty well – apart from the day when I was moved to staple his hand to the desk. Alarmingly he responded by smiling like a nun with concussion for the rest of the day.

Working on this book has furnished many surprises. I was thrilled to discover that the grumpy pundit we see on television is not the real Pat Spillane. Behind that tough mask is a generous soul. This was most evident on my birthday when Pat bought me a beautiful gift, which I will treasure forever. It was a signed copy of the acclaimed book *Self-esteem for Dummies*.

True friends stab you in the front.

John Scally,
November, 2004

1

Standing on the Shoulders of TV Giants

I suppose a lot of people would describe me as a perfectionist. A perfectionist is one who takes great pains – and gives them to everyone else!

When I retired from playing in 1991, I never expected a new career to open up for me as a pundit with the *Sunday World* and on *The Sunday Game*. I love it, but not everyone welcomes having a microphone stuck in his or her face. My team-mate on the great Kerry team, Ger Power, was once asked a question in the build-up to a big match. He replied, 'Whatever I said last year, put me down for the same again this time.' To me, the media is a home from home. Mind you, it can get hot in the kitchen at times! The ultimate job in life is to get paid for doing your hobby. The next best thing is to get paid for talking and writing about your hobby and I'm lucky in that respect.

All of us who have reached the top of our chosen sport are immensely vulnerable when our gifts, and as importantly the drama they create, begin to fade, when the rest of our lives may loom like a dreary anticlimax. The problem when you retire is that you lose all power to influence a game. When you are a player, you can read reports in the paper about games, and think that you can change things, but once you stop that power is gone. As the years go by, the mind stays the same, but the body is very different. The great thing about being a pundit for most former sports stars is that it gives them a great outlet for continuous involvement in their game. Live television is like a trapeze act without a net below. On live television the adrenalin is really flowing and the heart beats a little faster, like it did before playing a big game. There is a huge gap, and I mean *huge*, in a player's life after he or she retires, and broadcasting fills that void somewhat.

I know I should be thankful for this second career and I really am. However, to a lot of people it would seem that that is not the case. At various times, I have annoyed every county in the country. Football fans in Kildare, Mayo, Roscommon and every county in Ulster are at the top of a very long list of those who have let me know of their unhappiness with my analysis. Former Liverpool manager, Bill Shankly, said that his full back, Tommy Smith, would raise an argument in a graveyard. The same comment could be made about me! The pundit in general has a long and not entirely honourable tradition in sports broadcasting and journalism.

Wired for Sound

Sport is so popular now that only a tiny fraction of those who would like to get the opportunity to attend All-Ireland finals or rugby internationals can get tickets. Hence the importance of television, as it is now the medium through which the vast majority of people have access to their favourite sports. Indeed some sports, like snooker, owe their popularity almost entirely to television exposure. New satellite technology brings even more opportunities. Despite all the incredible advances in technology, television is not everything. Most people, given the chance, prefer to 'be there'. From its earliest days, sport has been a great spectator attraction. The great Roman architects laid out their stadia, not just for the Russell Crowes and Charlton Hestons of their time as gladiators and chariot-racers to showcase their talents, but to create 'atmosphere'.

George Bernard Shaw once said: 'Men trifle with their business and their politics; but never trifle with their games. It brings truth home to them.' From the earliest times there were people who reported on sporting events. Greek and Roman writers recorded many sporting events. In *The Iliad*, Homer recorded in considerable detail the games organised at the funeral of Patroclus. The attraction of sport is that it provides drama, tension, excitement, winners and losers, pain, laughter and sometimes even tragedy. Sport is uncertain, often to the very finish, (Remember the 1982 All-Ireland? And yes, it was a push in the back by Seamus Darby. Elephants never forget!) and it is intensely human. It makes headlines, it provides a good read, it makes for great pictures.

Television creates heroes and, as I have discovered at first hand, anti-heroes! Muhammad Ali was the first true world star of the TV age. Paul Gascoigne's fame soared after the 1990 World Cup, not because of his skills, but because he struck an emotional chord in the massive, worldwide TV audience for shedding tears on the pitch when it looked as if a yellow card from the referee might rule him out of the World Cup final. Within months Gascoigne was endorsing a wide range of products, many outside football including board games, deodorants, jewellery, calendars, to name just a handful. He also had a hit record even though he has a dreadful voice. Mind you, that's not a unique achievement! Even losers can find temporary fame and sometimes fortune through the universal appeal of sport, as the disastrous British ski jumper Eddie 'the Eagle' Edwards has shown in recent times. Sports stars have been used to endorse products since 1947, when the English cricketer Denis Compton, a kind of James Bond figure, became the face of Brylcreem. His face and slicked down hair became one of the best-known pictures in Britain, used in magazines and on billboards all over the country.

Television has, however, created its own problems for sport. Back in 1983, Sir Dennis Follows, Chairman of the British Olympic Association, observed:

> *We have now reached a stage where sport at top level has become almost completely show business with everything that one associates with show biz; the cult of the individual, high salaries, the desire to present a game as a spectacle – with more money, less sportsmanship, more emphasis on winning.*
> *All this has come through television.*

The following year Jack Nicklaus observed: 'Television controls the game of golf. It's a matter of the tail wagging the dog.'

Sport is vicarious living. It is tense, immediate, glamorous. Television generally (Gaelic games is something of an exception) pays large sums of money to bring the drama and entertainment of the major sports events into our homes. Sport is so popular with television companies because they are acutely aware that nothing stops the world in its tracks more effectively. In relative terms, compared with many other forms of entertainment such as film, sport is cheap. The bustling cities of Ireland were ghost towns when the boys in green were playing in the World Cup finals. Scarcely a bus moved on the streets. Sport is hugely important to television companies because it generates a large viewing audience. As such, it is a powerful weapon in the ratings war.

An example illustrates my point. It was not until 1964 that the BBC initiated what was to become the hallmark of British soccer coverage for an entire generation – recorded highlights on *Match of the Day*. ITV was quick to respond and started *The Big Match* on Sunday afternoons, featuring recorded highlights of one of the previous day's top games. For the first time, British viewers were given the benefit of expert analysis to complement the action. The BBC had the advantage of having no commercial breaks. To give them the edge over the Beeb, ITV invested Stg£60,000, which was a massive sum in the 1960s, in a slow-motion machine.

By the World Cup of 1970, when national interest was high and England's chances of retaining the trophy supposedly even higher, ITV boldly announced that it had discovered 'the formula'. A panel of provocative experts would enliven half-times and post-match discussions through a combination of informed comment, passionate debate and full-scale abuse. Malcolm Allison, Bob McNab, Pat Crerand and Derek Dougan – 'the two goodies and the two baddies' – sought to establish ITV's credentials as a legitimate alternative to the BBC in bringing soccer to the television audience. The science, using the term loosely, of football punditry was born. At home in Kerry, although I didn't realise it at the time, a new career was being created for me!

Paralysis by Analysis

From the outset, television pundits have had a history of extending the boundaries of the English language. As a number of them have struggled to keep their brain and tongue in tune, they have also spawned an explosion of 'Colemanballs'. The word 'Colemanballs' comes from David Coleman, a broadcaster whose name is synonymous with sporting howlers. The BBC commentator is remembered for a series of gaffes of which the following are but a tiny sample: 'This man could be a dark horse.' 'The late start is due to the time.' 'He's 31 this year; last year he was 30.' 'The pace of this match is really accelerating, by which I mean it is getting faster all the time.' 'One of the great unknown champions because very little is known about him.' 'Some names to look forward to – perhaps in the future.' 'Her time was 4 minutes 13 seconds, which she is capable of.' 'This could be a repeat of what will happen at the European Games next week.' 'This race is all about racing.' 'David Bedford is the athlete of all-time in the 1970s.' 'It doesn't mean anything, but what it does mean is that Abde Bile is very relaxed.' And finally: 'There is Brendan Foster, by himself, with 20,000 people.'

There are times as a viewer when I end up more confused than enlightened watching some of these pundits. Occasionally it is like watching a famous scene from the TV series *The Sopranos* when mafia boss Tony Soprano and one of his minders, Bobby Bacalla, are talking.

Bobby: The world really went downhill since 9/11. You know, Quasimodo predicted all of this.

Tony: Who did what?

Bobby: You know, the Middle East. The end of the world.

Tony: Nostradamus. Quasimodo's the hunchback of Notre Dame.

Bobby: Oh, right. Nostradamus.

Tony: Nostradamus and Notre Dame, that's two different things completely.'

Bobby: It is interesting that they'd be so similar, though. You know, I always thought: 'Ok, you got the hunchback of Notre Dame. But you also got your quarterback of Notre Dame.'

Tony: Notre Dame's a f**king cathedral!

Bobby: Obviously, I know. I'm just saying. It's interesting, the coincidences. What, you're gonna tell me you never pondered that?

I'm sure that there are many people who would compare me to Tony Soprano, because they would say my mouth is a weapon of mass destruction! I would be very insulted, though, if someone compared me to Bobby Bacalla. Unfortunately some of the soccer pundits on the telly are exactly like him in the strange way they distort the language of Shakespeare.

It is interesting, nevertheless, to see the way, down the years, ITV have poached some of the BBC's analysts like Ally McCoist and Ruud Gullit. This reminds us how serious a business is sport. It illustrates that punditry has become a powerful weapon in the sports ratings war. In Ireland it is a war that RTÉ has been winning hands down.

The Dunphy Show

Those RTÉ viewers who lived in single-channel land were first introduced to football analysis via *Match of the Day,* which was shown after the *Late, Late Show* on Saturday nights. RTÉ has always been quick at spotting a good idea and, after a few tentative steps and certainly by the 1978 World Cup in Argentina, it was fast catching up with the stations across the water in the punditry stakes.

It was the 1982 World Cup, though, that really showed a star had been born in the way Eamon Dunphy went against the tide of virtual universal euphoria about the Brazilian team. He claimed that the stylish Brazilians were flawed because they couldn't defend properly. Italy went on to prove Eamon right. In the European Championships in 1984, Eamon was at it again. He consistently claimed that French superstar Michel Platini was 'a good player but not a great player'. This time, however, Platini proved Eamon wrong. The point, though, is that everyone was talking about Eamon, and that is what a television station prays for. Mind you, Eamon himself took umbrage and went off in a huff when the late, great Dermot Morgan did a sketch on him after one of the games.

A good quality in any pundit is irreverence. Dunphy also scores highly in this category. In 2002, when speculation was rife as to who would replace Mick McCarthy, Dunphy was asked if he'd like the job. He replied, 'I'd love to do it but I couldn't afford the wage cut.'

Not all pundits are like Eamon, though. I watch football on ITV and BBC, as a lot of people in this country do, and there's nothing insightful being said. I've spent years listening to questions and answers on ITV like the following:

Dickie Davis: What's he going to be telling his team at half-time, Denis?

| **Denis Law**: | He'll be telling them that there are forty-five minutes left to play. |

The BBC equivalent is:

| **John Motson**: | Well, Trevor, what does this substitution mean tactically? |
| **Trevor Brooking**: | Well, Barnes has come off and Rocastle has come on. |

It is difficult to believe that some people get paid to utter banalities like that. It is not surprising that, during the 1986 World Cup, a letter was published in the *Guardian* on the subject of Mike Channon and Emlyn Hughes's performances as World Cup pundits. It made a plea from the heart regarding the lack of substance in their analysis: 'Conjugate the verb "done great": I done great. He done great. We done great. They done great. The boy Lineker done great.' The RTÉ audience though will not accept such inanities and rightly so. With Dunphy and his co-panellist John Giles there's no danger of that.

Giles was the midfield general at the heart of Leeds United's great success in the 1960s and 1970s, and is universally recognised as one of the greatest players of his generation.

During Italia '90, Dunphy became something of a national hate figure. It's a role I am very familiar with as the GAA's Public Enemy Number One. After the dreadful Egyptian match when Ireland drew 0–0, Dunphy appeared to go too far and anybody who saw it will never forget his annoyance. However, he was misrepresented in what he was supposed to have said. He was supposed to have said 'I'm ashamed to be Irish'. What he actually said was that he was ashamed of Irish football on the day and in the way the team played. He reacted very strongly to it, though, which created a lot of controversy. In doing this, the message was lost along the way as all the talk was about Dunphy's annoyance rather than what he actually said. Again I can identify with his experience because I am regularly misquoted, misrepresented and misunderstood.

Season of Sundays

Gaelic games have been at the heart of broadcasting in Ireland from its earliest days. On New Year's day, 1926, '2RN', Ireland's national radio station, began transmitting. On 29 August of that year, a Gaelic game transmitting live for the first time. The All-Ireland hurling semifinal between Kilkenny and Galway was the first radio commentary of a field game outside America. When RTÉ television came on air in 1961–2, the GAA initially adopted a cautious approach, restricting annual television coverage to the two All-Ireland finals, the two football semifinals and the Railway Cup finals on St Patrick's Day. Over the years, however, the GAA has spotted that television is not a threat but a useful ally in attracting people to our national games.

The year 1979 will forever be remembered as the year the Pope came to Ireland. It also marked the first transmission of *The Sunday Game*, a rare programme then devoted exclusively to Gaelic games. Popular Galway-based journalist Jim Carney and Seán Óg Ó Ceallacháin were the first presenters. Seán Óg's contribution to Gaelic games is well known because of his varied career as a Dublin county footballer and hurler, referee, sports commentator and reporter. In fact, so associated is he in the popular mind with Gaelic games, that people have great difficulty believing that he has an interest in any other sports. This was memorably demonstrated when a caller to RTÉ Radio Sport rang to ask about Manchester United. The conversation went as follows:

'Is this Seán Óg?'

'It is indeed.'

'Seán Óg Ó Ceallacháin?'

'The one and the same.'

'Off the radio?'

'That's me!'

'Sure what the f*** would you know about soccer?'

Seán Óg had a good team behind him in RTÉ, with Maurice Reidy as editor and John D. O'Brien as director. They made the brave decision to have Liz Howard as one of their main analysts. Liz was an All-Ireland camogie player brought up in a hurling household; her father was the great Limerick All-Ireland star Garrett Howard. For years she was PRO for the Tipperary County Board. In 1979 Liz hit the headlines following her comments about the Leinster football final on *The Sunday Game*. Legendary Dublin full-forward Jimmy Keaveney was sent off for a foul on Offaly defender Ollie Minnock. Liz was in no doubt that the sending off was very harsh. The next day the *Irish Press* carried the headline: 'TV personality supports Jimmy Keaveney' over a front page story. Keaveney was asked to attend a meeting of the Leinster Council Disciplinary Committee to explain his actions. The Dublin County Board invited Liz to attend the meeting and give evidence in support of Jimmy. She did and so did Ollie Minnock, who pleaded for leniency on Keaveney's behalf. Their pleas for mercy fell on deaf ears and Keaveney was suspended for a month, ruling him out of the All-Ireland semifinal against Roscommon. On the day of the match, Liz was going into Croke Park when she was accosted by a big Dublin fan who shouted at the top of his voice: 'Look at her. She's the wan who shafted Jimmy Keaveney.' It shows the hazards of being an analyst. You just can't win!

In 1997 Liz Howard made headlines again. Following Clare's victory over Tipperary in the epic Munster final that year, Anthony Daly made a speech in which he said, 'We're no longer the whipping boys of Munster.' A massive cheer went up from the Clare supporters when he uttered these words. To the consternation of everyone in Clare, Liz wrote in a newspaper article that the statement was 'conduct unbecoming'. Liz spent most of her youth living in Feakle, where her father was the local sergeant, so her comments hit a nerve, especially in her former home village. However, when she repeated this 'conduct unbecoming' theme two weeks later, the whole thing spiralled out of control. Other newspapers picked it up and it became a major controversy.

It is for me an interesting parable about the power of the media because shortly afterwards a man came to the door of Anthony Daly's shop in Ennis and said, 'You shouldn't have said that.'

Daly replied, 'What did I say?'

'Well, I don't know. But you shouldn't have said it.'

I can readily identify with Daly's experience. No matter where I go, I get people slagging me for things I said about their team and, in particular, things I'm *supposed* to have said. The best of all came two years ago when I met an officer of the Kilkenny County Board in Nolan Park and he said in all earnestness, 'What have you got against us? You're always slagging off the Kilkenny football team.' That was a new one on me! I have never even seen the Kilkenny football team playing, so I don't know how I could be criticising them all the time. People's memories often play tricks on them. They remember what they think you said rather than what you actually said.

Thankfully I grew up in the family bar. The interaction with customers from a young age sharpened my wits and prepared me for my subsequent career in the media in which I have to think quickly.

In the Beginning

Initially the chief football analyst on *The Sunday Game* was the late Enda Colleran who was a key part of the Galway three-in-a-row All-Ireland winning side 1964–66, captaining the side in the latter two years. Colleran was selected at right full-back on both the Team of the Century and the Team of the Millenium. He used the knowledge he acquired to telling effect as an analyst and blazed the trail for the rest of us to follow.

In Seán Óg's two years as a presenter, many players, both active and retired, were called on to give their opinions. The guest hurling analysts included Limerick's Eamonn Cregan and Pat Hartigan; Kilkenny's Pat Henderson, Eddie Keher and Phil 'Fan' Larkin; Clare's Jackie O'Gorman and Johnny Callinan; Tipperary's John Doyle; and Cork's Jimmy Brohan. The football guests were equally distinguished and included Kerry's Mick O'Connell and Mick O'Dwyer; Dublin's Kevin Heffernan; Antrim's Kevin Armstrong; Cork's Eamon Young; Mayo's Seán Flanagan; Cavan's Jim McDonnell; and Down's Seán O'Neill and Joe Lennon.

Another panellist in 1979 was Dave Weldrick. That year Dave had trained the Thomond College football team I played on and steered us to All-Ireland glory. While man-management mightn't have been his forte, as a coach he was a brilliant organiser and excellent at tactics. He applied the principles of soccer to Gaelic football. I remember him organising a training session with the senior team on the same day as the All-Blacks were having a training session on our grounds. We trained in opposition to the All-Blacks and they were on an adjoining pitch. The All-Blacks attracted a huge crowd, but before the end of their session they stopped their training and came over to watch us.

Because Dave was so technical, however, the jargon he used as a TV analyst went over the heads of 95 per cent of the population. And as he wasn't that well known as a player, unlike the Enda Collerans on the panel, he did not have the same credibility with the audience.

Down through the years, *The Sunday Game* has evolved and become indelibly imprinted in the national psyche, with Michael Lyster becoming the main presenter. The programme does not happen in a vacuum, with the match and analysis. There is a complex and highly professional packaging operation designed to convey a more attractive and seductive context for the event. The packaging begins from the very first minute with sophisticated graphics, evocative and carefully chosen music, as well as judiciously chosen and lively filmed images. These establish a mood of anticipation of an exciting programme to come. Powerful and dramatic opening sequences will almost certainly attract marginal viewers to certain sports.

One of the reasons why *The Sunday Game* has prospered is that the production team is always on the lookout for new analytical talent. On the hurling side, it brought in the greatest hurling manager of the 1980s, Cyril Farrell. Some people in Galway were disappointed that he continued to work as an analyst with the programme during his second coming as Galway manager in the mid-1990s. Their point was that it is hard to hunt with the hare and hunt with the hounds. Donal O'Grady, Thomas Mulcahy, Pete Finnerty and Michael Duignan are among a number of great former players who have made an invaluable contribution to the programme.

In the 1980s and early 1990s, Kilkenny's dominance of hurling ensured a bleak time for Wexford. This was most obvious on the Wexford side of the New Ross bridge, which separates counties Kilkenny and Wexford. A sign on the bridge read: 'You are now entering a Nuclear Free Zone.' A Kilkenny fan added a message of his own: 'You've now entered a trophy free zone.'

All this was to change with the arrival of one of hurling's great evangelists, Liam Griffin, as Wexford manager. Of course, hurling fans will never forget the way he steered Wexford to that All-Ireland in 1996. When he stepped down as Wexford manager, it was inevitable that his services as an analyst would be in great demand and RTÉ audiences have had the benefit of his passion for 'the Riverdance of sport'.

With his knowledge of the game, Griffin quickly became the Alan Hansen of co-commentary. In a world where words are cheap, the only pity is that Liam's sharp intelligence and clear elucidation could not be deployed by cross-channel stations for their soccer half-time discussions. Often the brightest thing about their analysis is Terry Venables' jacket.

Liam is a great raconteur and has remarkable energy. I saw this at first hand in the Burlington Hotel on the morning after RTÉ's Sports Personality of the Year awards early in January 2004. There was a virtual who's who of Irish sport walking around the hotel. Most people were still bleary-eyed from the night before. I was sitting down having my breakfast when Liam came over to me full of vim and vigour. He told me that at one of his first meetings with the Wexford panel he gave them a questionnaire to fill in. It had a number of questions such as: 'Where would you prefer to train?' At the bottom was an additional query: 'What is your favourite position?' Most players answered in the obvious way, 'full-back, centre half-back, full-forward', etc. The exception was a new panellist to *The Sunday Game* this year, the joker from Faythe Harriers, Larry O'Gorman, who gave Griffin information he didn't really need. His reply was simply, 'On top!'

When Liam had finished that story, Mick O'Dwyer passed by us. As soon as he saw Micko, Liam launched into the story of how, in 2002, he attended a social function with the then Dublin manager, Tommy Lyons, and Micko, who was Kildare manager at the time. At one stage, Tommy said to O'Dwyer, 'Micko, you and I will fill Croke Park this year.' O'Dwyer replied, 'Tommy, you and I wouldn't fill a toilet!'

A bit of humour is great in a presenter or analyst. That's why someone like Des Lynam is so popular. He's got some great one-liners like: 'There's Frank Leboeuf and his son le Spare Rib.' His best, though, was probably: 'Our experts tonight are two guys who between them have won 106 caps for Scotland. Kenny Dalglish who has won 104 and Bob Wilson who has won two.'

From Clare to Here

For many people, the most memorable moment on *The Sunday Game* came on the night of the 1997 All-Ireland final, after Clare narrowly beat their old rivals Tipperary. Former Limerick player and manager Eamonn Cregan was one of the guests on that programme. Following Cregan's analysis the cameras went live to Clare's celebrations at the team hotel and to the Clare manager, Ger Loughnane. Loughnane began his response with the comment, 'After that ten-minute whinge from Eamonn Cregan ...' He then launched into an attack on Cregan. Given the intensity of Loughnane's comments it seemed, even to outside observers, that there must have been some history between them. Loughnane had been on the Clare team in 1983 when Cregan was training it. Loughnane did not rate him as a coach and, in his eyes, Eamonn was definitely the wrong man to come on and criticise Clare, considering he had had no success there. Loughnane was standing beside Ger Canning during the interview. Canning sensed that the Clare crowd was aghast, so he looked Loughnane straight in the eye and said, 'That's terrible isn't it?' Loughnane replied, 'Pay no heed. That's only Cregan.' Then he let fly! It is a revealing insight into Loughnane's personality that his only regret is that he didn't 'tear' into Cregan more strongly that night!

I was not in the least surprised that following his retirement as Clare manager, Ger was brought on *The Sunday Game* as an analyst. Loughnane is now the classic poacher turned gamekeeper as a weekly columnist with *The Star* newspaper and as a perceptive and articulate interpreter for *The Sunday Game*. As a disciple of the John Giles, rather than the Trevor Brooking, school of analysis, he pulls no punches, is animated, intense at times, and maintains a flow of relevant information and interpretation.

For media bosses the temptation to plunder the thoughts of former star players and successful managers, and benefit from their judgements is overwhelming, particularly when, like Loughnane's and mine, their name has become the touchstone for controversy. After the famous Loughnane interview on Clare FM in 1998 at the height of the Colin Lynch controversy, someone remarked that Loughnane cost Irish industry £25 million because workers were constantly talking about him when they should have been doing their jobs!

First we had the cult of the manager, now we have the cult of the pundit. The Meehan brothers were the powerhouses of Caltra's first ever All-Ireland football club title on Saint Patrick's Day, 2004. The Friday night before the game, most people in Ireland were watching the *Late, Late Show* to see the four remaining members of Westlife talking about coping with life after Bryan McFadden's departure. The Caltra team, though, had invited a special guest to talk to them about coping with Croke Park for the first time – Ger Loughnane.

Ger brings some of the qualities he showed as a player to his job as a pundit. In the 1976 League final replay, Eddie Keher suffered a head injury and the blood was pumping out of him, necessitating a long delay while he got attention. Loughnane, ever helpful and compassionate, went up to him and said, 'Jaysus Keher, would you ever get up and get on with it. Sure there's nothing wrong with you!'

The Earley Years

Funnily enough you don't see as many current players acting as analysts now as you used to. In the late 1980s, for example, Paul Earley was a regular analyst on *The Sunday Game* even though he was still playing for Roscommon and had been an All-Star a few years before. He worked well because he matched his deep knowledge of the game with a bit of humour. One of his best moments came after the 1988 All-Ireland semifinal when Mayo, managed by John O'Mahony, put up a credible showing before losing to mighty Meath. At the end Michael Lyster asked Earley, 'Will Mayo be back?' Quick as a flash Paul replied, 'I hope not!'

Colm O'Rourke has been an analyst since 1991 when he was still the best player in the country. In his autobiography, Liam Hayes deals with the ripples of discord that were created on the Meath panel back in 1991 when he joined, but O'Rourke has been an inspired choice and to this day is one of the best pundits you will find anywhere. His mind is as agile as an Olympic gymnast. When he talks about football he nearly always seems, quite simply, to hit the right note. You can't ask any more of an analyst than that. Mind you, Brian Dooher would probably disagree! Colm also comes up with some good one-liners. Last year, as Armagh's focus and obsessive will to win a second All-Ireland looked all-consuming, O'Rourke's incisive observation was: 'If Adam was an Armagh footballer, Eve would have no chance. Instead of an apple, he would have looked for a banana, as this is on the diet sheet.'

Former players and managers like Martin Carney, John Maughan, Bernard Flynn, Tony Davis and Tommy Lyons have all played their part as analysts. Kevin McStay has brought a new terminology to football analysis, using terms from basketball like 'pops'. The likes of John Joe O'Reilly, when listening in to him from that great football pitch in the sky must wonder what he is talking about. However, one of the most colourful analysts on RTÉ is Joe Brolly, one of the greatest characters in the history of the game.

One of the many stories Brolly tells is of his experiences playing against Meath, and marking Kevin Foley in particular. A high ball came in between them, Brolly fielded it, and in his own words, 'danced around' Foley and blasted the ball over the bar. A second high ball came in between them with exactly the same result. Brolly was aware though that the Meath crowd had gone very quiet and noticed Foley and Liam Harnan exchanging signals. When the next ball came in, Brolly could see both Foley and Harnan coming at him at top speed so he ducked, causing

Harnan to catch Foley with his elbow. Foley was stretchered off unconscious. Brolly claimed that he became a hero in Derry, not because off any score he ever got, but because he was the man who 'floored' Kevin Foley!

As you can imagine that story did not endear him to Colm O'Rourke, who said, 'Joe Brolly always talked a great game. The problem was that he didn't always play a great one!'

After his retirement as a footballer, Brolly turned his considerable talents to working in the media. Joe is very comfortable in that environment but his desire to be brutally honest has not always been appreciated, especially by Tyrone fans! A typical Brolly comment is: 'Why don't sharks attack Pat Spillane? Professional courtesy.' That kind of craic makes working on a panel all the more enjoyable. The panel that laughs together works well together.

It is also good when panelists have a bit of an edge to their comments. I would not be the biggest fan in the world of the BBC soccer coverage, but I did enjoy Martin O'Neill's comment to Gary Lineker during the last World Cup: 'You know what I like about you, Gary? Very little.'

Having been a great player in the past does not necessarily make a person a good pundit. A prime example of this is Sir Bobby Charlton. Given his fame, he was in great demand by broadcasters. The problem was that he was too nice a guy. He was worried about the feelings of others and would never attack anybody. As a result, he was very bland. In marked contrast, his brother, Jack, was a great pundit because he was honest and always gave forthright answers. A good example of this was when he was assessing the Holland–Germany game on ITV during the 1990 World Cup when Frank Rijkaard and Rudi Voller had what is euphemistically called in GAA parlance a 'shemozzle' and Rijkaard spat at his opponent. Jack was asked what he would have done if Rijkaard had done that to him. Without blinking an eye, Big Jack replied: 'I'd have chinned him.'

The Inside Track

For those personalities who have retired from playing, media involvement affords them the platform to continue their happy addiction to the small and large dramas created by players when they suspend accepted reality in favour of a private, if heightened, version of it on the pitch. As television pundits, our task is to inform, enthuse and to entertain, drawing on the depth and authenticity of our experiences.

This is where a good pundit comes in. To be a good analyst, you must put aside your own prejudices or allegiances and report on the facts. Anyone who does not do that is failing as an analyst so you do have to learn the tricks of the trade. I would compare TV punditry to playing at the highest level. You've got to have experience and grow into the job. It is a very technical medium. Timing is everything on television. You only have a limited amount of time to put your point across and then you have to shut up. I absolutely cringe now when I look back at some of my early appearances on television. I should have remembered that it is better to keep your mouth shut and appear stupid than to open it and remove all doubt.

I was invited by RTÉ to compete in their inaugural Sports Superstars Championship to be recorded early in 1979. I joined Limerick hurler Pat Hartigan; footballer Dave O'Leary; swimmer David Cummins; Formula One driver Derek Daly; athlete Noel Carroll; Dublin footballer Jimmy Keaveney; boxer Mick Dowling; and Cork's Jimmy Barry Murphy. To give a light touch to the proceedings, the sports personalities were divided into teams each made up of two 'superathletes', one female athlete, one personality and one politician. Personalities who agreed to take part included Fr Michael Cleary, Frank Kelly and Dickie Rock. After I won the competition, I took part in the World Superstars competition in the Bahamas. I did not know much about protecting myself from the sun and as a result of my pink visage and body, a new phrase entered popular currency, 'the Pat Spillane tan'! When I think of how I looked and the things I said back then I am mortified.

Former players like me have been through the 'slings and arrows of outrageous fortune' that a serious career in sport necessarily entails. We know what it's like to suffer uncomplimentary newsprint. I've lived through the pain of experiencing a shock defeat and walking away afterwards with my head still shaking at the ground in anguished disbelief. I know the feeling of just wanting to get on the bus, and having the frustration of a journalist shoving a mike in my face and asking the sterotypical stupid question: 'What are your feelings on the game?'

Given the amount of heartache and pain I suffered coming back from an injury that I was told would finish my career, I can completely relate to the type of dedication that causes a top jockey like Tony McCoy to live solely on a diet of chicken and Jaffa Cakes. I understand why Herb Elliot, the 1500-metre Olympic champion from Australia, retired at the incredibly tender age of 21. He hung up his spikes because he had never been beaten over his Olympic distance and was unsure how he would handle the trauma when it inevitably came. To outsiders these competitors are not of this world, but for those of us who have competed at the highest level in our chosen sport, or as Macbeth would have put it, acquired 'the sickness', we all think we are madly normal. We live and breathe the game. We know why second best is just not good enough. We know that it is the small things that make the big differences. A lot of the time winning is not about being 100 per cent better than your opponents, but about doing 100 things one per cent better than the other team. We know that in the lead up to a big game, you want – no you need – an atmosphere as reassuringly familiar as the odours of home cooking. We understand how the hours peel away like layers of insulation before a match, and we can decipher the throb of misgiving that can be detected in strident predictions of success. We have gone through what Sir Clive Woodward calls the T-Cup or Thinking Correctly Under Pressure.

Being an analyst does mean that we have to comment on friends, for example, after the 2002 and 2003 debacles I had to be critical of Kerry, managed by friend and former team-mate Páidí Ó Sé. It is not easy for anyone to be critical of a friend. When I was playing with Páidí, we both did everything we could for Kerry to win. Now though, as analyst and columnist, I am there to comment on what happens as it happens. I'm not there to sit on the fence. Whatever has to be said, I'll say it. I'd be selling myself, those players, or those reading or watching short if I wasn't fully honest. It doesn't mean I respect Páidí any less. Anyone who has ever been involved with me would say that I always gave an honest assessment of what happened in a match whether it be victory or defeat. I'm continuing in that vein as an analyst. Sometimes, however, telling it as it is can cost you friends. People may remember that Mick McCarthy, early on in his days as Irish manager, refused to be interviewed on RTÉ television by Jim Belgin because of some of Belgin's comments in the analyst's chair. People want you to analyse and give your honest opinion. I find now that over a period of time people accept you. If I say now somebody played well or played badly, generally people know that I mean it. If I pandered to the public every time I commented on a match, people would soon see through me.

The job of a pundit, to steal shamelessly from Robert Frost, is to provide what is demanded of a good poem, 'not necessarily a great clarification ... but a momentary stay against confusion'. I think a good analyst reacts to the game rather than imposing a kind of excitement on it. I don't really enjoy the Gary Newbon school of breathless touchline interviews. I watch Sky Sport, but I think it's dishonest when they have, let's say, Hull City versus

Bristol Rovers playing a dull 0–0 draw and their pundits use language like 'thrilling encounter'. That doesn't serve the audience, and ultimately an analyst's job is to serve the audience.

The ingredients of a successful pundit are an in-depth knowledge, a love for the game that knows no limits and an unfailing ability to convey the flow of a match to equally satisfy the needs of the cognoscenti and those at the opposite end of the spectrum of sporting knowledge. To quote Rudyard Kipling, we must find a very particular balance:

If you can talk with crowds and keep your virtue,
Or walk with kings – nor lose the common touch ...

That Mr Kipling writes exceedingly good poems!

You also need a calm authority because on live television during fast-changing events when things are not going to plan, you can't make a drama out of a crisis. My job is to make the watching public feel part of the event, part of the team. You have to be able to introduce a common touch to arenas which some viewers find inaccessible, like the tackle in Gaelic football.

As an analyst my job is also to pull no punches when it comes to dealing with the issues of the day. My role affords me the platform to be a thorn in the side of those in authority. I was a player for a large number of years. I see where the deficiencies are. I see where the cracks are now. Unless they are faced up to, football will be in big danger. Officials are there to serve the game so that it can be handed on to future generations. If I think they're not doing their job, I am going to point it out. That doesn't make me popular with them!

To quote wee Daniel, or is it Jim Reeves? *Welcome to my world.*

2

The Top GAA Riddles

Q: Why do the Dublin footballers ride ladies' bicycles?

A: They have difficulty getting their balls over the bar.

Q: What's the difference between the Wicklow football team and the Ryder Cup team?

A: There's only one langer on the Ryder Cup team.

Q: What's the difference between Ryan Giggs and Pat Spillane?

A: Ryan Giggs is the best winger around. Spillane is the biggest whinger around.

Q: Who were the last two Westmeath men to play midfield in the All-Ireland final?

A: Foster and Allen.

Q: How many intelligent Cork fans does it take to screw a light bulb?

A: Both of them.

Q: What's the difference between God and Pat Spillane?

A: God doesn't think he's Pat Spillane.

Q: What's the difference between a dead dog on the road and a dead Meath fan on the road?

A: There are skid marks in front of the dog.

Q: What do you have when Pat Spillane is buried up to his neck in sand?

A: Not enough sand.

Q: You're trapped in a room with a tiger, a rattlesnake, and Pat Spillane. You have a gun with two bullets. What should you do?

A: Shoot Pat Spillane twice.

Q: What do the Derry football team and Frank Bruno have in common?

A: They're both out after round one.

Q: What's the difference between an aspirin and Ger Loughnane?

A: An aspirin will cure your headache. Ger Loughnane will give you a headache.

Q: Why do Meath make football a colourful game?
A: Everyone ends up black and blue.

Q: What's the difference between the Longford goalie and Pamela Anderson?

A: Pamela has got two big assets in front of her.

Q: Why is Gaelic football different from sex?
A: One involves sensuality, passion, emotion, commitment, selflessness, the speechless admiration of sheer heart-stopping beauty, rushes of breathtaking, ecstatic excitement, followed by shattering, toe-curling, orgasmic pleasure. And the other is sex.

3

The Men Behind O'Dwyer

My job as an analyst begins every year at the RTÉ Sports Personality of the Year awards programme. An integral part of the show is to have a panel of pundits from different sports reviewing the previous sporting year and looking forward to the next one. It's usually George Hook, Liam Griffin, Ted Walsh, Eamon Dunphy or Brian Kerr, and myself. It is good television and RTÉ like to get a bit of friction going.

In the first year, after I had made some point, Hook went off on a typical rant. Ted Walsh intervened and said that we were missing the point of sport. He argued that sport was about the Olympic ideals and in that perspective it was not the winning but the taking part that counts, and that the true spirit of sport is captured by the Special Olympics. It was a very populist thing to say and Ted lifted the roof with audience applause. Ted had driven the boot into Hook and myself, and afterwards we wondered if his wealthy owners would have been happy if he approached horse racing with that Corinthian attitude.

The next year Hook and I decided that we must get Ted back because he had had a cut at us the previous year. The only problem with that strategy is that Ted is as slippery as an eel, and it is very hard to get a dig at him. Undaunted I waded in and said I was watching the Kildare County final on the television the previous Sunday, and that I thought the team that won, Kildoran, was woeful. Ted went on a rant and I soon fell foul of his tongue.

He famously said to me, 'The real problem with the foot-and-mouth epidemic, Pat, was that you didn't get it.' The only thing was that Ted added two and two together and got five. What I was referring to was the RTÉ series *On Home Ground* which was set in Kildare, and based around the fictional football team, Kildoran. Either Ted didn't watch the series and didn't know what I was talking about, or else he knows very little about club football in Kildare.

The Morning After the Night Before
In 2004 Ted came to us before the programme and told us he wanted a truce.

The programme reflected the fact that 2003 had been a disappointing year for Irish sport. That was brought home to me when Barry Geraghty was voted Sports Personality of the Year. Of course, Barry had had a great year, is a wonderful jockey and has had stunning achievements on the track, but I suspect that if you were to do a vox pop of most Irish people, not a lot of them would know who he is.

The morning after the 2004 awards ceremony, I woke up with the mother of all hangovers. It could have been worse. The same night Britney Spears got married while under the influence. What galls me to this day, though, is all the people I had spoken to that night and how I can't remember a single thing they said. I spoke at length with John Delaney of the FAI. He told me the real story of what happened in Saipan. I spoke for ages with Louis Kilcoyne about the real story of what happened to Shamrock Rovers in Milltown. I talked with Eamon Dunphy and he explained in great detail to me why his television show had failed. The only thing I remember very clearly is that he was very unhappy about a former Kerry footballer and manager who appeared not once but twice on the programme, but who had failed to sparkle on either occasion. I spoke at length with Pat

Devlin about his role in Damien Duff's transfer to Chelsea. If I could remember all these conversations I'd have enough for four books.

Through bleary eyes I scanned the newspapers. All the attention on the sports pages was on Páidí Ó Sé in his first match at the helm in his new role as Westmeath manager. It was the day of his first competitive match in the O'Byrne Cup. I was talking with a friend of mine who had met Páidí the day before when he was out walking. Páidí told him that Westmeath 'were playing some match tomorrow', but he didn't know what competition they were playing in. At least Páidí's luck is changing. The referee played an extra seven minutes against Louth and Westmeath had time to score a winner.

As I struggled to eat my breakfast that morning I met Mick O'Dwyer. I marvelled at his enthusiasm. At 66 years of age, he was about to head off to Dromard in Longford for a Mickey Mouse match in the O'Byrne Cup. What was bugging him? Martin Delaney couldn't play that day. Mick has the ebullience of a ten-year-old.

George Bernard Shaw once said there were two classes of people: the equestrian class and those who disliked horses. He might well have said the same thing about all sport. If the need is for a little philosophical justification of the irrational enthusiasms that keep so many of us in thrall to Gaelic football, of the romantic resilience that sustains us, then I must concede defeat from the outset. A former, albeit not very distinguished, Gaelic footballer, Patrick Kavanagh, argued that all sporting subjects are 'superficial' as 'the emotion is a momentary puff of gas, not an experience'. I know there's absolutely no way I can rationally explain to any non-football fan why the sight of two groups of men chasing up and down a field after a bag of wind can cause someone's heartbeat and blood pressure to go absolutely crazy. The passionate intensity of someone like Mick O'Dwyer defies rational analysis.

Mysterious Ways

There are three kinds of people in this world; those who can count and those who can't. In my career as an analyst there have been two constants. If you are a GAA pundit it is a fact of life that you will spend a lot of time talking about referees. Referees are intrinsically involved in the sweat and the rancour of the game. Sometimes they do the job well, but often they don't.

We all make mistakes. After I qualified as a teacher and was established as a Kerry player, I wrote to RTÉ Sport, applying for a job. Weeks passed and I was dismayed and bewildered that I did not receive a request for an interview. Finally, six months later, I received a message from RTÉ that explained why I hadn't heard from them. It read: 'Your CV was not attached as stated. I do, however, want to thank you for the Kerry match programme.'

I understand that referees will make mistakes, but what really annoys me is their inconsistencies. While the standard of refereeing has improved considerably in recent years, there is still a long way to go. The GAA should stop worrying about Mickey Mouse offences, such as having your socks down around your ankles, and concentrate instead on ensuring that all the rules of the game are applied consistently by all referees.

Some things never change, however. Since time immemorial, football fans have been complaining about referees. In fact, a recent archaeological find in Kerry uncovered ancient scrolls of a series of conversations between a caveman from Tralee and his wife. At one point the caveman said, 'I'm still annoyed about watching that match today. The referee was a w****r.'

In frustration his wife shouted at him, 'Will you ever get off your arse and do something productive like discover fire.'

The second constant is my perpetual bewilderment that Mick O'Dwyer has never been appointed manager of the Irish team for a Compromise Rules series against Australia. This year, yet again, he was snubbed. Why those in power constantly overlook him is a bigger mystery than the third secret of Fatima.

When he was the chairman of the Kerry County Board, Seán Kelly was the most vocal critic when Micko was overlooked for the manager's job on previous occasions. When he became the first Kerry president of the GAA, every one of us thought that at long last the oversight was going to be corrected. Not so. Seán, everyone in Kerry wants to know why O'Dwyer did not get the job. Is it because he is not the best man for the job? If so, come out and say so. Tell us what more he needs to achieve before he is worthy of this honour.

Seán was quoted as saying that O'Dwyer's commitments with the Laois team would prevent from giving his full attention to the Ireland job. Yet Pete McGrath was tied up with a club team in Louth, Cooley Kickhams, until the end of September, while O'Dwyer had been resting for two months at that stage. Pete's deputy, John O'Leary, was managing the Dublin Ladies team until the start of October.

Mick was very, very disappointed when he was passed over as the manager of Ireland's first team for the Compromise Rules series in Australia in 1986. Instead the job was given to Kevin Heffernan. O'Dwyer was also disappointed when the team captain for that series, 'one of his own' Jack O'Shea, publicly praised Heffo. Kevin did an excellent job and I don't want to take that away from him. But the fact remains that O'Dwyer was very hurt.

O'Dwyer felt, however, that the next time the job came around he would get it. In actual fact he had asked me if I would be involved with him and I was looking forward to that, but he was passed over yet again in 1987, this time in favour of Eugene McGee.

To be manager of your country is the ultimate prize, it is the icing on the cake, the final glory. This year Micko was deprived of that distinction again and it was absolutely scandalous. O'Dwyer is not the sort of person to publicly say it, but I know deep down he is hurting. It is a joke that as a sop he was offered the job of assistant manager with the possibility of him taking the top job in two years. You don't do that to a man of 66 years of age.

Pete McGrath, the choice as manager, is a gentleman, but he has no experience at international level. Then they appointed Larry Tompkins as his assistant and John O'Leary as his second assistant. Tompkin's record as manager was woeful and O'Leary's was even worse!

Leave It to Mr O'Brien

Who does O'Dwyer compare with in management terms? The only Irish sportsman I can compare him with is Aidan O'Brien. At first sight Aidan O'Brien, bespectacled and unassuming, is cast in a different mould than O'Dwyer. Little wonder Aidan was once compared to a Trappist monk. Yet the comparison misleads more than it elucidates. Few monks have the *savoir-faire* to become a serial champion trainer. A more helpful comparison might be with O'Dwyer; both have a passionate obsession to win and win and win again. There is more to these men than meets the eye.

O'Brien does his talking on the racetrack and in the record books. He has the determination, the obsession, the single-mindedness, and a passion untrammelled, steely and pure that one could not help but admire. Like Cliff Richard, he does not look his years. A few years ago, a prospective owner arrived in Ballydoyle for a scheduled appointment. O'Brien was doing casual work in the yard and was dressed like a stable boy. The stranger asked him, 'Where's the trainer?'

Long before Ger Loughnane came on the management scene, O'Dwyer was a great man to pull a stroke. In the late 1970s we used the hand pass a lot. At one point people started to complain that we were using it improperly and were gaining an unfair advantage as a result. O'Dwyer was concerned that it would cost us dearly in an All-Ireland final if we were penalised for not using it properly. So before the match he invited Paddy Collins, who was to be the referee for the big game, down to Tralee for one of our training sessions. O'Dwyer had each of us doing all kinds of hand movements with the ball and every time he would ask, 'Is this okay, Paddy?' Each time Collins would nod his head. When it came to the match, we did what we liked with the hand pass because we knew Collins couldn't penalise us because he was the one who showed us how to use it.

O'Dwyer could be the archetypal cute Kerry hoor. Whenever he thought anybody was watching us train who might be on a spying mission, he had us play soccer. However, in the interests of cultural purity it was never called that. He referred to it as 'ground football'.

Both O'Brien and O'Dwyer are great students. Dwyer can recognise when a player is right just by looking at him. People who know tell me that one of O'Brien's greatest strengths is that he knows when a horse is right.

We reap what we sow. The turning of the world depends on countless unsung heroes going about their business of earning a quiet living. But the salt in the soup is provided by exceptional people who take risks for no more fundamental reason than it reminds them that they, and the rest of us, are alive not dead. Aidan O'Brien and Mick O'Dwyer are such men.

Let's Get Physical

O'Dwyer and Laois were in the headlines early in 2004 when they lost the first three matches in the League. O'Dwyer was not panicking because at that stage he had not started training properly with the team yet.

The great thing about O'Dwyer, and one of the many reasons I admire him, is that he is his own man. He doesn't ask advice from anyone. When he started training the Kerry team, he had at least five PE students/teachers on the team. We were fellas who knew more about fitness, hamstrings and injuries than he did, but he never once asked our advice. The first time the GAA public heard of a hamstring was when Bobby Doyle pulled one in the 1970s.

O'Dwyer's recipe for success is very simple. The formula has never changed. In winter it consists of laps of the field: 10 laps, 14 laps, 20 laps – laps upon laps. Why laps? It is very simple. There are two reasons. First, it builds up stamina. Second, you find out the character of the players on the side, because the fellow who will sweat blood on the training pitch will also do so in a game. With this strategy he produces teams that are exceptionally fit and that are just right on the day.

Nowadays, players have diet plans and schedules for the gym. In our time when we won the All-Ireland, we stopped training in September and we weren't seen again until March or April. There was a lot of subterfuge in the reports of our lack of training, however. While we were not training together, each of us was training on our own. Micko did have a problem with what were termed 'the fatties' on the team who put on weight like John Egan and the Bomber. He would bring them back earlier for extra training. He would always have a few rabbits or hares to set the pace for them. The interesting thing, though, was that there never was a complaint from Egan or Liston.

O'Dwyer's final year with Kerry came in 1989 after three successive defeats to Cork in Munster finals. That year he thought he could get one last hurrah out of the team. It is probably the six million dollar question for a player or a manager coming to the end of his or her career: is there one last kick in the team? That year O'Dwyer felt the only way he could eke out one last title from us was if we were all really, really fit. He had us training in a little all-weather track in the Kerins O'Rahilly pitch in Tralee. We ran and we ran and we ran. It is one of the rare mistakes he made. Unfortunately all of our energy was left on the training field and, when it came to games, we had nothing left in the tank.

So Sad to Watch Good Love Go Bad

That period coincided with my marriage. I used to teach in Bantry, arrive home and cover for my wife in the family bar while she had a break for her dinner. Then I'd go and train savagely hard with O'Dwyer in Tralee. Kerry were cost-cutting at the time so it was only sandwiches after training. When I got home from training, I would go back in to give my wife a break from working in the bar. I remember one night going upstairs, jumping into bed, knackered to the world. A few minutes later my wife slipped seductively into bed beside me. Her hand came over. That's the sort of thing that happens with newly married couples. She should have expected the right reaction from a willing partner. In this case though it wasn't an amorous response from a newly-wed husband but a crocked, wrecked victim of Mick O'Dwyer's training regime who proceeded to tell her, 'Forget about it. I'm banjaxed. Go away. Don't even dream about it.'

With that came the quick retort: 'If Mick O'Dwyer wanted you to do it – you'd do it.'

You know what. She was probably right.

I told that story afterwards to Gay Byrne on the *Late, Late Show* and she was sitting in the front row. Everyone who saw her afterwards said she looked mortified. She was, and I had literally to pay a high price. The next day I had to take her shopping!

Nostalgia Is Not What It Used to Be

Nostalgia can be a dangerous pastime when it clouds the memory and impedes our ability to recall accurately the strands of the past. When offering opinions about Gaelic football today, I am sometimes criticised that I am forever harking back to the past, and to the great Kerry team that I played on. Maybe I do. I suppose we are all guilty of eulogising about our own era at the expense of the present day.

When it comes to comparing standards from one generation to another, the pundit who is an ex-player is always on difficult ground. It is easy to lose track of the boundary between proud self-belief and triumphalism. Training methods, tactics, diets and general preparation for the game have altered dramatically from when Mick O'Connell stopped playing in 1974. It makes it almost impossible to make judgements on how players from the distant past would have performed had they played in a different time. There are players, though, who would have prospered in any era. They had that X factor that set them apart in their own dreams. They had the vision, determination, imagination and, above all, the sheer skill to rise above the players around them. I am sure that Jack O'Shea *et al* would do just the same if they were playing today.

What would also have made those Kerry players stand out in any era is that they were an exceptionally intelligent bunch. Their speed of thought was most evident in the way Mike Sheehy cleverly chipped Paddy Cullen with a quick free, which turned the 1978 All-Ireland final in our favour. After Seamus Darby's sensational last-minute winner for Offaly against Kerry in 1982, that Mike Sheehy goal is the most famous ever scored in an All-Ireland final. Paddy Cullen's frantic effort to keep the ball out was memorably described afterwards by the legendary Con Houlihan, who wrote that it was like 'a woman who smells a cake burning'.

I was just watching the tape of the goal recently and I heard Michael O'Hehir describe it as 'the greatest freak of all time'. You would have to take him to task for that comment. It was a moment of pure genius in the speed of thought and the execution of a very difficult skill. Absolutely magnificent. Of course it wasn't a free. But that's beside the point.

I can honestly say that there are no group of people I admire more than the members of the Kerry team. I have to be honest, though, and say the love affair is not entirely reciprocated. When I wrote my autobiography a number of years ago, I wasn't prepared for the kind of reaction it provoked, especially from what I thought was the most innocuous chapter in the book on my team-mates on the Kerry team. I had gone through the chapter carefully and did not think that anybody would take offence at any part. I had a little section of comments on each of them, talking about their playing abilities and so on. I really didn't think I could have upset many people, but I did. There are several who although they have continued to talk to me since the book came out, have shown a definite coolness towards me.

The one player who won't talk to me is Ogie Moran. A few years ago there was a special function in Tralee to honour the great Kerry team. I went to shake hands with Ogie, but he turned his back on me. When we line up in parades in Croke Park, he won't talk to me and he won't shake my hand. I believe, though, that sticks and stones will break my bones, but neither words nor silence will ever hurt me.

Ogie was a great player. He had to be to win eight All-Ireland medals, all of them in the centre half-forward position. He had great skill, outstanding speed and total unselfishness. My problems with Ogie, or more precisely his problems with me, go back to the time when he was manager of the Kerry team and I was very critical of him. Ogie is a lovely fella, but was not cut out for management at all. He had a poor Kerry team picked and made poor decisions on the sideline. I quite rightly criticised him and his selectors for that, but the important thing was that I wasn't criticising him because it was Ogie, I was criticising him because he wasn't doing what I thought was best for Kerry football and that infuriated me. I was simply giving my opinion as that is what I'm paid to do. Talk is cheap and I'm the first to say I'm sorry, but the bottom line is that I felt I called it as I saw it, but Ogie hasn't spoken to me since. This is something that saddens me. Life is short. Much too short to be bearing grudges.

One of my dearest wishes would be that Ogie and myself could bury the hatchet. There is nothing I'd like more than for Ogie to give me the opportunity to pass him the peacepipe.

Mind Games

There are those who believe an intelligent Kerry footballer is one whose IQ is higher than his shirt number. Mick O'Dwyer is not one of them. I'm not saying Micko is the best manager of all time, but there are none better!

It was not that he was great on tactics. He wasn't, but like sex, the movements in Gaelic football are somewhat limited and predictable and tactical genius isn't everything. Micko's real talent was that he was a great man-manager.

It is difficult to keep a positive attitude in the face of criticism or negative feedback. Negatives sometimes seem more powerful than positive feedback. So O'Dwyer always told us that we were the best. Before big games we never concentrated on the opposition, we just focused on our own game. The great leader is the one who encourages others to rally to the cause, and O'Dwyer had that gift. Hopes rise, hopes are crushed. It will always be thus. But there is one abiding, redeeming feature which all sport shares. New every morning, the hopes are there. However, motivation becomes tougher after success. It is like climbing Mount Everest. Once you have reached the summit, it is very hard to motivate yourself to do it again. The motivation to win the first All-Ireland was obvious. Getting the team to draw from the well a second time and then again and again was a whole new challenge, but the old seductive dream of gaining glory kept coming knocking on the Kerry team's door time and time again.

The suspicion persists that Kerry footballers secrete some kind of archetypal fluid that makes it easier for them to win football games than players from any other county. That's a load of nonsense. We would have won at least three All-Irelands without

O'Dwyer because we had so many talented players, but we would not have won eight. He kept us wanting to come back for more.

As I said, O'Dwyer's key to success was man-management. He made you feel that you were the greatest. His other secret was motivation. He realised early on that medals weren't the thing, so he had to find other carrots to dangle. He started with holidays and then moved on to better holidays.

We're All Going on a Winter Holiday

Exotic tours abroad were a feature of O'Dwyer's motivational tools with the great Kerry teams of the 1970s and 1980s. It has left me with many wonderful memories. In 1986, O'Dwyer brought us on a holiday to the Canaries. It was mainly for rest and recreation but there was also a small element of training. Every evening at 5 pm, the players met for a run along the sand dunes of Playa de Ingles. As we ran towards Maspolomus part of the beach was reserved for a nudist's section. I noticed that when the Kerry players reached that section of the beach on their run, the pace dropped alarmingly!

Four years earlier, O'Dwyer brought us for a run on a beach in San Francisco the day after we had given a horrendous performance against the All-Stars. The display was the legacy of a day-long drinking session by some of the squad at Fisherman's Wharf on the eve of the match. The most revealing evidence of the commitment of the Kerry players' to the cause was that the first man home on the beach run was the current president of the GAA, Seán Kelly, then Chairman of the Kerry County Board.

An apocryphal story told about the experiences of the Kerry team on tour illustrates a more generous side of our nature. The Bomber Liston had many admirers, including one young lady from Australia, who engaged him in idle conversation.

'Scuse me, are you the Bomber?' asked the attractive, blonde Aussie. The Bomber nodded his assent.

She responded with an obvious comment: 'You know you are one hell of a big man.' Again the Bomber nodded his head.

As she barely reached his bellybutton, she gazed wistfully over his manly charms and asked, 'Are you all in proportion?'

He was forced to admit he was not. The light died in her eyes, only to be rekindled when he replied, 'If I was in proportion, I'd be 6 feet 10 inches.'

In 1981, after completing the historic four-in-a-row of All-Ireland titles, we went on the holiday of a lifetime to America, Hawaii and Australia. We were booked into a hotel in Adelaide in Australia after a long overnight flight. Shortly after we arrived, an irate member of the Kerry delegation rang down to complain about the lack of air conditioning in his room. He threatened to pull the entire Kerry party out of the hotel if the problem was not fixed immediately. A member of staff arrived up to the room and took a quick glance around, before looking the man with a complaint in the eye and coolly saying, 'Why not try and plug it in buddy?'

In 1982, Kerry planned a holiday to Bali in the Far East to celebrate what we had expected to be our five-in-a-row. After sensationally losing the final to Offaly one of the lads said that the only Bali we would be going to was Ballybunion! Another said, 'It won't even be the Canaries this year. All we'll get is the seagulls.' It has been said that we didn't underestimate Offaly in 1982 – they were just better than we thought!

With a Little Help from My Friends

Micko has always had a great talent for getting good people to help him out. He got the great Micheál Ó Muircheartaigh to train the Kerry lads in Dublin. However, Micheál's skills were also in demand in other areas. In 1983, Jack O'Shea was the Kerry captain. Kerry had won the Munster final every year since 1975, and in 1983 most people expected us to win again. Jacko worked on his victory speech with Ó Muircheartaigh and they were very happy with it. The only problem was that Kerry lost the match. Jacko's great speech was never made.

There was another twist to the story. Kerry forgot to bring the Munster Cup with them and it was only quick thinking by Frank Murphy that saved the day. He searched a press in the back room and found some cup – apparently the Cork Junior Championship trophy. That's the cup that was eventually presented to the Cork captain, Christy Ryan, but nobody seemed to notice.

Micheál Ó Muircheartaigh is one broadcaster who is universally loved. He is completely free from the pretension associated with many of his colleagues. Not for him the nickname given to one of his peers, 'the Ego has landed'.

Few people have done more to promote the whirr of the flying sliotar and the thrilling sound of ash against ash than the voice from Dingle who makes GAA fans tingle, Micheál. To shamelessly steal from Patrick Kavanagh, among his earthiest words the angels stray.

Micheál has left an indelible mark on the GAA landscape with a series of classic comments:

'Pat Fox has it on his hurl and is motoring well now ... but here comes Joe Rabbitte hot on his tail ... I've seen it all now, a rabbit chasing a fox around Croke Park.'

'Pat Fox out to the forty and grabs the sliothar ... I bought a dog from his father last week, sprints for goal ... the dog ran a great race last Tuesday in Limerick ... Fox to the 21, fires a shot, goes left and wide ... and the dog lost as well.'

'A mighty poc from the hurl of Seán Óg Ó hAilpín ... his father was from Fermanagh, his mother from Fiji, neither a hurling stronghold.'

'Teddy looks at the ball, the ball looks at Teddy.'

'In the first half they played with the wind. In the second half they played with the ball.'

'1–5 to 0–8, well from Lapland to the Antarctic, that's level scores in any man's language.'

'I saw a few Sligo people at Mass in Gardiner Street this morning and the omens seem to be good for them; the priest was wearing the same colours as the Sligo jersey! 40 yards out on the Hogan stand side of the field – Ciaran Whelan goes on a rampage – it's a goal. So much for religion.'

'... and Brian Dooher is down injured. And while he is down I'll tell ye a little story. I was in Time Square in New York last week, and I was missing the Championship back home and I said, "I suppose ye wouldn't have *The Kerryman* would ye?" To which, the Egyptian behind the counter turned to me and he said, "Do you want the North Kerry edition or the South Kerry edition?" ... he had both ... so I bought both. Dooher is back on his feet.'

Micheál is much more than a sports commentator. He is a national institution. As we march, not always successfully, to the relentless demands of a faster, more superficial age, just to hear his voice is to know that all is well with the world. Although he has dabbled in television, his real forte is radio where he paints pictures with words like a master craftsman. Young boys listening to him decide immediately that they want to join the ranks of the football and hurling immortals. Irish sport would not be the same without him. He is irreplaceable. Seldom has one man brought so much joy and inspiration to so many. If enthusiasm was electricity, Micheál would have been a power station. He is quite simply *the* voice.

The Boss

Mick O'Dwyer had a kind of aura about him that made players want to earn his favour, and a completely natural, straight-from-the-heart sense of how to inspire players. He was able to bring the best out of his gifted but sometimes difficult stars. Micko's rule was law, the more demanding of obedience because it was given in a soft, kind, reasonable way against which it was impossible to argue.

O'Dwyer takes the Gucci view about hard work on the practice field – long after you have forgotten the price, the quality remains. He thinks footballers are like tea bags – you have to put them in hot water before you know how strong they are.

His one fault is that he is stone mad for money. Someone said if Micko got money for his wife he'd sell her. They were only half wrong!

Micko is a loveable man, driven by football. Football is in his blood. It is his fix. He is Kerry to the bone's marrow. Radio Kerry did a poll to find the Kerry person of the century. Sr Consilio won it, though most people believe she was born in Cork. Tom Crean was second. You couldn't quibble with his selection. Micko was third, Dick Spring came fourth and Daniel O'Connell was fifth. I found it interesting that Dick Spring was ahead of Daniel O'Connell. Obviously getting someone a council house or a medical card was more important than getting Catholic Emancipation.

In Dublin 4 everyone is into image and having their celebrity status acknowledged. It is very different in Kerry, and rural Ireland in general, where you are never allowed to get too many notions of grandeur, or in fact *any* notions of grandeur. You keep your feet on the ground.

My father-in-law told me the story of an American film crew who went to Iniskeen to make a documentary on Patrick Kavanagh. When they visited the local pub, they expected a great reception after they announced their mission and went out of their way to state publicly: 'Patrick Kavanagh was a great poet.' The wind was taken out of their sails when one of the locals replied: 'Ah sure there's a man down the road, Peter Bunting, who could poetry the sh*te out of Kavanagh.'

However, it was probably after he left Kerry that Micko's true prowess as a manager was revealed, notably when, in his first year, he steered Laois to a Leinster final after decades in the wilderness. Even though they lost their Leinster crown in 2004 and even if they collapse in 2005, O'Dwyer will still have a job for life in Laois. I do believe, though, that somewhere down the line again he would like to manage Kerry for one last time. It would be the final piece of the jigsaw.

In his exilic period after leaving the Kerry job in 1989, Micko first made his mark with Kildare. At that stage Kildare had reversed their policy of changing their trainers frequently. In fact, in the 1970s, they seemed to have a different trainer every year. At the time it was suggested that they had more trainers than Sheik Mohammed!

From the outset Micko faced a serious problem. He recognised that he had a problem because the Kildare forwards could not hit a bull's arse with a banjo, so he got them to play to their strengths which were fitness, short-passing and a running game. If they had succeeded in getting Declan Browne or a top-class forward, he would have won an All-Ireland with them.

There was only one time I had reservations about O'Dwyer's methods. I remember meeting him after Kildare's second drawn game in the epic trilogy with Meath in 1997. As usual, the Kildare forwards had been generally kicking the ball everywhere but between the posts. Micko told me that he had brought the Kildare team in for extra training that night and that Pat McCarthy had them down to the Curragh, and that he was going to, 'run the sh*te out of them'. I thought to myself that they would be better doing the extra training somewhere with goalposts and loads of footballs, and they should be practising getting the ball between the posts.

Despite their lack of a top forward, O'Dwyer brought the glory days back to Kildare, taking them to a Leinster title after a 42-year gap. Who will ever forget their comeback against Dublin to win the Leinster in 2001? Their best chance of an All-Ireland came in 1998, but Galway were too good for them on the day.

Mr Unpopularity

Down the years my relationship with Kildare supporters has been incendiary! After my comments about the shortcomings of their forward line in 2001, in particular, I was their most despised man on the planet. A rash of Pat Spillane jokes appeared on the websites of clubs all round Kildare.

One of the stories was about the day my daughter brought home her report card. I was supposed to be very displeased and said, 'Why can't you be more like Mary Sparks? She's always at the top of the class.' 'But Dad,' my daughter said, 'you have to remember, she's got really smart parents.'

Another has three Kildare men kidnapping me, pinning me down in a dark alley and giving me a dice and saying, 'If you get a 1, 2, 3, 4 or 5 you're dead!' So I asked, 'What if I get a 6?'

The Kildare lads said, 'You get another go!'

For some inexplicable reason they also cast aspersions on my tact and sensitivity. They tell of a woman who walked on to a bus with her child and the bus driver said, 'That's the ugliest child I've ever seen.' The woman sat down beside me feeling very offended. She told me about the incident with the bus driver and told me she was going to complain. 'Fine', I said. 'I'll mind the monkey.'

Another story relates to the bookshop in Naas that decided to stock condoms. Many young people were embarrassed to be seen buying condoms in public, and when they got to the counter often changed their order at the last minute to a book. One day an earnest young seminarian in Maynooth, who knew nothing about football, went into the shop to buy my autobiography. When he got to the counter there was a stunningly beautiful girl at the counter. The young man lost his nerve and blurted out, 'Can I have three packets of condoms please?'

Revenge is a dish best served cold. In response to these comments, all I will say is that I hear that a Kildare supporters' help-line has been opened, the number is 1800 1–nothing, 1–nothing, 1–nothing.

4

The Top 10 GAA Books that Will Never Be Written

The long winter nights are a time for putting your feet up and reading a good book. The quality of GAA books on the market varies dramatically, but here's a list of 10 books you won't see for sale this or any other Christmas.

1. *How to Score a Free from 40 Yards* by the Dublin forward line

2. *The Beauty of Ulster Football* by Pat Spillane

3. *Aren't Tyrone Footballers Great?* by Joe Brolly

4. *My Glory Days with Dublin* by Tommy Lyons

5. *The Art of Successful Forward Play* by the Kildare forward line

6. *How to Win Friends and Lose Enemies in the GAA World* by Ger Loughnane

7. *Brian Dooher: The Authorised Biography* by Colm O'Rourke

8. *101 Ways to Get Around the GAA Rule Book* by the Cork County Board

9. *My Aversion to Publicity* by Páidí Ó Sé

10. *How to Train an All-Ireland Winning Team* by Larry Tompkins and John O'Leary

5

Observe the Sons of Ulster Marching On

This has been the most difficult chapter of this book to write.

During the spring of 2004, I decided to devote 48 hours of my life to writing nice things about Ulster football. After two days of taxing my brain like never before, I looked down at the page and it was still completely blank.

That reminds me of the story of the late Maurice O'Doherty, who was one of the most famous people in Ireland when he read the 9 o'clock news on RTÉ television. He was very laid-back and came in to read the news at a minute to nine each night. One evening Maurice was finishing the news when he came to the weather. He looked at the page and it was blank. Maurice, being the true professional that he was, said: 'And the weather will continue for the next 24 hours.'

However, during the summer as the Championship unfolded, like St. Paul before me, I found myself on the road to Damascus. Thanks to the wonderful displays of Fermanagh this year, I have seen the light! I have radically rethought my attitude to the Ulster counties.

I realise that my fears in 2003 about the direction the Ulster counties were taking Gaelic football were misplaced. In fact, far from seeing them as the enemy, we should be on our knees in gratitude because they have dramatically raised the standards for others to emulate, and as we saw from Kerry in the All-Ireland final, the standards have been surpassed.

Back in the 1980s, there were a lot of pious platitudes about Ulster football, but once they started winning regularly, maybe there was some resentment that they didn't know their 'proper place' anymore.

However, let me first explain why I was so anti-Ulster football before.

Public Enemy Number One

The former Dunfermline player Jim Leishman once said: 'I was the first professional football player to be forced to retire due to public demand.' I know what he means. If Ulster GAA fans had their way I would be off the telly in no time. So why have I such a bad history with them? There were six reasons for my antipathy towards Ulster football.

First, it was a physical thing, particularly in the 1990s. Take Armagh, for example. My illustrious colleague Colm O'Rourke said of them: 'Armagh are hard in every sense of the word. They live a bit on the edge, blocking runs for return passes, staying in the dressing-room at half-time and feigning injury at times …'

One of Micheál Ó Hehir's favourite euphemisms was: 'And it looks like there's a bit of a shemozzle in the parallelogram.' Had he been commentating on Ulster football in the 1990s, he would have had to come up with some new phrases.

In fairness this is not a disease that afflicts only Ulster football, but it was certainly very prevalent there. Part of the reason for this is that the rivalries between the counties are so strong.

In the maternity ward of a hospital, a Tyrone fan, a Derry fan and a Rastafarian are sitting beside each other. A doctor comes in and says, 'Congratulations. All three of you have just become first-time fathers. I'm delighted for each of you. There is one slight problem. With all the frenetic activity that has taken place here in the last few hours, we are not exactly sure which baby is which.'

With that the Derry man raced in to the ward and grabbed one of the babies and took him away. The baby he chose had dark skin and dreadlocks. The doctor ran after him and said, 'Excuse me, sir. I wouldn't have thought that baby belongs to you.'

The Derry man replied, 'One of the other two is from Tyrone and I'm not prepared to take any chances.'

Beauty and the Beast

My second basis for disliking Ulster football was for aesthetic reasons. Gaelic football at its best is the beautiful game – played with strength and speed, courage and skill, honesty and humour. It has the capacity to stop your heart and leave the indelible memory of a magic moment. Think back to a footballing artist like Matt Connor – in full flight he was something unbelievable on the pitch, a miracle of speed, balance and intense athleticism, a thoroughbred leaving in his slipstream a trail of mesmerised defenders who had been as transfixed in wonder as the crowd by his silken skills. This is why I wanted to play the beautiful game.

I am reluctant to use the word 'puke', but at its worst Gaelic football is like watching Tyrone beat Kerry in the 2003 All-Ireland semifinal. A perversion of the beautiful game like that is like measles; it is something you should get over young, not at my stage of life. Football should leave you looking frenzied, looking mad with joy. Much Ulster football in recent years had simply left me simply looking mad. It is watching muck like this that is causing me to grow old disgracefully.

I got sick of watching games in Croke Park where the only performers trying to play positively were the Artane Boys band. I blame the puk ... negativity in Ulster football on video analysis and blanket defences. The problem that comes with video analysis as a tactical weapon is that it doesn't concentrate on your own strengths but on the opposition's. Over the last few years in Gaelic football, we've aped what's been going on in Rugby

League and Rugby Union, and Ulster teams in particular seemed to spend most of their time trying to figure out ways of counter-acting the opposition rather than playing to their own strengths.

With Mick O'Dwyer we never, ever, ever discussed the opposition: their style of play, their key players or their tactics. We moved the ball quickly. It was a very simple philosophy. We didn't look at the O'Neills on the ball, but were instructed to be aware of what was going on around us and move the ball quickly. The only time we used video analysis in my time as a Kerry player was in 1991 when Mickey O'Sullivan was in charge. We looked at several videos of the Down team before playing them in the All-Ireland semifinal, but the thing was that on each video they were winning, and the more you watched them you more you thought they could beat you.

Back in 1979, the Buggles raced to Number One with the song 'Video Killed the Radio Star'. I think there has been signs of video killing a generation of sports stars as it encourages negativity and focuses on curtailing the opposition from playing their game. I have been longing for the innocent days of Gaelic football when one team beat the other team by scoring more than them. To achieve this, I proposed as a first step that all match videotapes should be destroyed. Instead of worrying about the opposition, coaches should revert to the basic philosophy of sport: trying to score more than the opposition. Unfortunately, it sounded like a pipe dream in this cynical day and age. Kerry, to a significant degree, has brought the good old days back again in the manner in which they won the All-Ireland this year. They have revived the traditional values of catching and especially kicking the ball. One swallow doesn't make a summer, but hopefully the negative tactics of 2003 will be consigned to the dustbin of history.

We are even importing the language and methods of rugby into Gaelic games. When I was playing I never heard anyone talking about 'taking hits', but today players speak that language all the time. I found it interesting that after Meath lost to Laois in the Leinster semifinal in 2004, they did a session with the Bradford Bulls in Dalgan Park. A day or two before the Munster hurling final, I was talking to the former Cork hurler Tomás Mulcahy, who had been at a Cork training session the night before. He described one of the drills as follows: two players went into a square ten yards by ten yards, and their task was to pass the ball to each other. Two lads with tackle-bags were placed on one edge of the square and two more on the other, and their job was to chase down the lads with the ball. I have since found out that the Kerry football team also use tackle-bags in training.

A thing we have imported from soccer is something the Waterford hurlers did repeatedly this year, which was holding up the crest of the jersey when they got a score or made a good catch or whatever. It is supposed to be a sign of loyalty. I am very suspicious of it. The soccer player who did this most conspicuously this year was Alan Smith of Leeds. Within two weeks he had signed for Leeds United's most hated enemy, Manchester United.

Thou Shalt Not Pass

My second proposal in an effort to make football more aesthetically pleasing, is that blanket defensive systems be outlawed. After Kerry lost to Tyrone in 2003, Seamus Moynihan incisively observed: 'The midfield area was like New York City, like going down Time Square. Crazy.' In this approach, nothing is left to chance. Success seems to be based on a platform of defence and safety first. Keep possession, keep mistakes to a minimum and play in a manner that allows skilful players only the least little bit of room and time to do their thing. Ulster football in the past subscribed to the belief that victory is based on getting defences right, players funnelling back, and slowly but surely choking individuality. The most worrying aspect of this tactical approach is that, while it is ugly and horrible to look at, it is both deadly effective and legal.

One way of counter-acting this blot on the face of humanity is by placing a big full-forward on the edge of the square. I'm fed up with seeing too many dainty, fancy forwards who need good quality ball and acres to perform their array of tricks. I long for the return of a Bomber Liston-type full-forward or even another Steven McDonnell to emerge. Basically, I'm looking for fellows who can win 50/50 balls, don't need a roundabout to make a turn, can give and take the hits, and most importantly of all, score. In the Connacht Championship match between Roscommon and Sligo in 2004, Roscommon's Karol Mannion showed, yet again, how effective this endangered species can be. The most obvious plan to bypass the blanket defence was illustrated by Kieran MacDonald in Mayo's victory over Tyrone – the first-time ball in quickly to the forward line.

The Winner Takes It All

The third reason why Ulster football frustrated me so much was that a win-at-all-costs mentality seemed to dominate. It wasn't always like this. Tyrone really gave Kerry a scare in the All-Ireland final in 1986. With a great display of positive football, they had us on the ropes. Early in the second half we trailed them by seven points. And it could have been worse, had Tyrone right-half-back Kevin McCabe not blasted a penalty over the bar.

Sport is a microcosm of society. If our language is part of who we are, our sports actually tell us who we are. When we know the way winners and losers are treated in sport and the way rules are enforced, then we know a great deal about the larger society in which it exists. Conversely, if we know the social, economic and political values of a society, we could make an inspired guess about how its sport is organised. Unfortunately when we talk about sport today, we must recognise that sport has a dark side. The defects we find in sport – cheating, violence and drug abuse – are an integral part of the wider society.

Increasingly sport is becoming identified with the culture of the survival of the fittest. This involves subordinating everything else in sport to winning. This approach was encapsulated in the popular saying attributed to the famous American coach, Vince Lombardi: 'Winning isn't all-important, it's the only thing.'

Ulster counties seemed to have adopted this attitude more than any others. Two stories illustrate the desire to win in Ulster football; one features a club side and the other fans. They show how this win-at-all-costs mentality has infected all facets of the game. In the early 1990s, a certain club in Cavan was playing an Intermediate relegation game. They fielded a ringer – a Meath county footballer who a few years earlier had won an All-Ireland senior medal. He played under an assumed name. He caught the ball on his own forty, went on a solo run and scored a sensational point. One of the opposition management said, 'Jaysus, that lad is brilliant. He should be on the county team.' The chairman of the opposing team muttered under his breath, 'He is.'

After Cavan lost to Tyrone a few years ago in an Ulster Championship match they should have won, the Cavan fans were dejected. Cavan's Cathal Collins had not had a good game, and as he trooped wearily off the field, the Cavan fans started shouting at him: 'They shot the wrong Collins.'

I got a great insight into the Northern mentality at my first function in the North. It was a question and answer session in Coalisland in the early 1990s. You have to try and realise that Northerners are coming at things from a totally different angle. I realised that when a fella put up his hand and asked me, 'Do you know why Jack O'Shea never catches the ball at the throw-in?' I was puzzled and said I did not. He continued, 'I'll tell you why. It is because Jacko has a contract with Adidas, a foreign company, and that's why he never catches the ball, in case he'd be photographed with it.' In the circumstances, after I got over my initial shock at the suggestion, I thought the politic thing to say was, 'You could be right.'

A personal experience of my own threw new light on this peculiar mentality for me. The Tyrone-based company Powerscreen sponsored the All-Star awards for a few years. In an effort to try and avoid some of the selection controversies, they decided to get the players to nominate the All-Stars. In the middle of November that year I was stuck for something to write in my column, so I wrote an article on why I thought it was wrong for the players to make the selection. My argument was that they would not have been in a position to see every player in the Championship, and more importantly, that some players are popular and some aren't, so nice guys had a better chance of winning it than hard men or guys who were unpopular with their peers. I thought that this was unfair. At that time of the year, when things are slow, the All-Star selection is a hardy perennial for any hard-pressed journalist stuck for something to write about, whether it is the selection process, the nominations or the final selection. I didn't think my article would have any repercussions because it was so innocuous. Not for the first time I was wrong.

I had formed a very good relationship with one of the senior staff in Powerscreen. After the article was published, he rang me to tell me that he wasn't very impressed with it. At first I thought it was a wind-up. I had the article in front of me and read it and asked him if he was serious. He emphatically assured me that he was. I said, 'I hope this is not going to affect our friendship.'

He replied, 'It already has.' He hasn't spoken to me since.

The Mini-skirt Factor

Ulster football managers have resorted to all kinds of devices in the quest for victory. One is an obsession with statistics. Everybody knows that Mickey Harte has two guys up in the press box taking statistics from the match. As Oscar Wilde famously said, there are 'lies, damned lies and statistics'. However, I think former Aberdeen manager Ebbe Skovdahl was even more accurate when he said, 'Statistics are like mini-skirts – they give you good ideas but hide the important things.'

Most people will remember that in the All-Ireland quarter-finals in 2003, Armagh kept Laois waiting for an age in Croke Park before they returned for the second half. Apparently the reason they were so late was because they were busy analysing the statistics. A good manager doesn't need statistics to tell him what his side are doing in training or in a match. Mick O'Dwyer doesn't need to be told that his side won four of the six kickouts on the left wing and six out of nine kickouts on the right wing.

While I think the current emphasis on statistics is way over the top, it would be equally foolish to ignore the fact that there are a few things we can learn from statistics. Statistics reveal that in the 2003 All-Ireland football final a mere 58 kicked passes were executed compared to 227 hand passes. May I respectfully suggest that if players, and particularly managers, want to get involved in a game that involves such a volume of hand passes, they should take up Olympic handball.

Another thing we can learn from statistics is the shocking number of stoppages there are in Gaelic football. On average, we get 40 frees in 70 minutes in the League and about 50 stoppages in the Championship. Throw in the natural breaks in play for scores, for balls going over the sidelines and endlines, and it is totally unacceptable that a game that should provide constant entertainment is stopped once every minute. I checked the statistics for games in the Premier League and the average number of stoppages for frees is 25, which means that if you allow for injury time, the referee goes for four minutes without stopping the game.

I applaud teams for doing anything that will give them an extra edge in a game, provided it is not at the expense of the basics of the game, that is, catching and kicking. Statisticians are dictating what coaches should do on the basis of statistics. Let us take one example for illustrative purposes, although I could take others. Statistics reveal that very few kicked passes from fifty yards reach their intended target. Statisticians tell coaches to play short passes. But why do passes go astray? It is simply because too few players can kick the ball accurately. My point is that the remedy for the problem is not to tell coaches they can't kick long, but to get them to practise kicking the ball long and straight. Thankfully, Kerry have made kicking an integral part of Gaelic football again this year.

I believe the buzzword in the modern game is turnovers. I am told that the moment that one of this year's All-Ireland semifinalists returned to their dressing-room at half-time, the first thing their manager did was to tell them they had won the turnover battle 8–4. This leads to a percentage game resulting in short hand-passing, a mazy series of diagonal and backward passes that makes you wonder if Brian O'Driscoll and Gordon D'Arcy haven't beaten the ban and sneaked into Croke Park after all.

Imitation Is the Sincerest Form of Flattery

There is a thin line between success and failure. When Clare hurlers made the breakthrough in 1995, early morning training became the new craze because that was one of the techniques Ger Loughnane pioneered. But had Seánie McMahon not won the sideline that led to the late goal against Cork in the Munster Championship, nobody would have heard anything about it. In 1996, when Wexford won the All-Ireland under Liam Griffin, camping out on Curracloe beach was the new big thing, and, of course, everyone heard about Griffin's masterstroke of having the team walk across the county border between Wexford and

Wicklow on the way to the match. The reality, though, is that had Limerick taken their chances that year, the McCarthy Cup would have spent the year on Shannonside and the rest of us would never have heard about the 'border crossing'.

When Armagh won the All-Ireland in 2002, they started wearing arm bracelets to keep them focused. They also started using inspirational speeches from other sports, like the one Al Pacino used in *Any Given Sunday* speaking to his American football team before the play-offs. He talked about how life is a game of inches and so is football because in either game, life or football, the margin of error is so small. When you look around you, you're going to see a guy who's going to go that extra inch with you, who will sacrifice himself for the team because he knows you're going to do the same for him.

The biggest thing everyone else aped was Armagh's idea of going on a trip abroad to a training camp. This year, for example, Mayo had a five-day training camp in the Catskills after playing New York, Kerry went to the Canaries, while Roscommon, Armagh and Monaghan went to La Manga for a training camp. In an interesting sign of the times, Monaghan sent a spy into the Armagh training camp! Meath went to Prague. I am pretty sure that after the way Meath lost to Laois in the Leinster semifinal, Prague will not be getting any repeat business.

This year everyone has been looking at the formula Tyrone manager Mickey Harte used last year, such as having no challenge games, which quickly became de rigueur for everybody else. Had Armagh got a goal near the end of the All-Ireland, however, when Steve McDonnell was clean through only for his shot to be blocked down by Conor Gormley, nobody would be talking about Mickey Harte's brilliant and innovative training methods.

Too many teams are like sheep. They follow the crowd. If one team does 100 laps a night, the next one has to do 120 laps. If one crowd train up a 100-metre hill, the next have to find a 200-metre hill and then the next have to climb a mountain. When one crowd goes for a swim in a pool, the next has to swim in a lake and the next go swimming in the sea.

I often think of what would have happened if Mayo had gone on to win the All-Ireland in 1992. They came within a whisker of beating the eventual All-Ireland champions Donegal in the semifinal. In a highly publicised saga afterwards, the Mayo players signed a petition which called for the removal of their manager Brian McDonald, and in the process, released a list of training methods that they had used during the year which seemed to border on the farcical. Only one side of the story was told in public. Player power saw McDonald bow out, with Jack O'Shea taking his place, only for Mayo to be absolutely massacred by Cork the following year in the All-Ireland semifinal. With a bit of luck, though, Mayo could easily have beaten Donegal in 1992 and who knows what would have happened against Dublin in the All-Ireland final. McDonald, being very cute, improvised when there was no field available for training by getting the Mayo lads to push cars around the carpark. If Mayo had won that All-Ireland, everyone would have said McDonald was a genius and car-pushing would have become part of the training manual for every team in the country.

The Beginning of the End?

Michael Jordan famously said, 'I've failed over and over again in my life, and that is why I succeed.' Failure can be a self-perpetuating misery chain, but equally it can be a tremendous motivator for success. Ulster football is making up with a vengeance for the years when it had little success. We saw this in some of the comments after Tyrone's All-Ireland victory in 2003. Tyrone boss Mickey Harte said, 'We had to work very hard for this – it took 119 years for us to get it.' As he lifted the Sam Maguire Cup, Peter Canavan said, 'They said we were like the

British Army, that we lose our power when we cross the border, but we've proved we have power today.'

In fairness, Peter was not the only All-Ireland winning captain to take a pot shot at the critics in his after-match speech. Dinny Allen famously did it in 1989. Although he didn't mention him by name, I think Mick O'Dwyer was Dinny's main target. My view, though, is that the only way to answer your critics is to win. When you do that you don't have to say anything. All you have to do is lift up the Cup. One of the phrases of the year was, 'We proved the critics wrong.' The classic example of it was the Waterford hurlers. They were desperate against Galway in the League final and yet were brilliant the following Sunday against Clare in the Munster Championship. After the Clare match, Justin McCarthy lashed out at 'the critics'. Critics make a judgement on known form, the last game or games. The pundits had backed Clare because Waterford had been dire the week before, it was as simple as that. Whenever I hear teams or managers going on and on about proving the critics wrong, I think it is a sign of insecurity.

Mind you, Fermanagh has revived the beautiful game up north again. Earlier this year I invited readers of my *Sunday World* column to send in their thoughts about the game to me. The first email I got was from a big fan. It read:

> There was this very good Gaelic football player who won an All-Ireland in 1975 as part of an exceptional team. As a member of the Thomond College team in the All-Ireland club seven-a-side in UCD in April 1978 and having been defeated in the final by Bryansford, he sobbed like a baby. Although he went on to win a further seven All-Ireland medals over the next ten years or so, still as a good player on an exceptional team, he could never be rated in the same class as Kerry's own Mick O'Connell, Down's Dan McCartan, Offaly's Matt Connor, or in modern times, Tyrone's Peter

Canavan. Based on his achievements he became a legend in his own mind and set himself up as the face of our National Games.

The second email came from Terry Rehill in Cavan. He told me about the philosophy of coaching he uses with his youngsters: 'Catch it like you love it and kick it like you hate it.' To illustrate that the ball is faster than the boy or girl, he lines up the kids and gets them to race the ball, that is, he shouts 'go' and kicks the ball as hard as he can up the field while the kids run up after it. Needless to say the ball always wins. Another innovation I liked is that he has also introduced the 'intelligent pass'. During training games he awards a point for a pass that will open up the play and speed up the game. It has resulted in kids having a look around when they get possession to see where they can lay it off to.

All GAA coaches take note.

When It's Not a Funny Old Game

The fourth basis for my aversion to Ulster football was that it was generally humourless. This was brought home to me on 29 January, 2004, when a documentary went out on RTÉ television called 'The Men Behind Maguire'. What really infuriated me was that after just two years of success, Ulster teams were telling the rest of us how to win the All-Ireland. Indeed it seemed to me that they were actually dictating to us the way the game needs to be played. Talk about bias and propaganda.

The only two southern voices the programme had on were Mick O'Dwyer and John O'Mahony. They both reserved judgement. Talk about fence-sitting. I would like managers to be more forthcoming in interviews. GAA managers should learn from Portsmouth's manager, Harry Redknapp. When asked about taking the post he replied, 'Why did I take the job? I was skint.'

In the documentary, Martin O'Neill couldn't understand why Ulster victories are criticised so much. The problem is that

Martin obviously hasn't been watching much Ulster football in recent years.

Tyrone and Armagh have been at the top in the last few years because they've put more into the game in recent times than any county in the 26 counties. I admire them for that. They deserve their success. However, as we have seen this year, Ulster's reign at the top was not as enduring as some people predicted. In recent times when I have gone up to speak in either Armagh or Tyrone I have always begun by congratulating them on their one-in-a-row. I then tell them that I speak as a member of the Kerry team that won the four-in-a-row between 1978 and 1981 and the three-in-a-row between 1984 and 1986. I then tell them as an afterthought that I too was part of a one-in-a-row in 1975, but that we don't bother counting that in Kerry. These comments always get a reaction!

One of the reasons why I wanted to write this book was to remind people that Gaelic football is still a game. It should be a leisure pursuit about craic and giving a bit of relief from the everyday pressures of life. I feel in the north they take football way too seriously.

What really scared me watching the documentary was that they had a clip of a group of young teenage lads in Tyrone who were preparing for a match. It reminded me of a pre-marriage course. It was way too serious. It was like they were being prepared to go into battle. Young footballers should be betrothed to fun, but these lads looked like they were attending a management course. This typified for me what Ulster football has become.

Away from the football fields and television studios my day job is as a secondary teacher in Bantry. I teach PE and Geography. All I ask from my students is that they do their best. I see my job as helping them to do their best. To me education is not just about getting exam results. What I want to do is to help to produce well-rounded young people. After five years in my care, I want them to leave school as good, solid, mature young people. When you are a parent, you realise how much of an act of faith it is to leave your kids in somebody else's care. Teaching is a huge responsibility. Naturally you want the very best for your own kids and it helps you to understand how parents feel when they entrust their children to you. As a result, since I became a parent I have worked harder at helping the students to get the best out of themselves. I wish people who coach juveniles would take that attitude rather than having kids obsessed about winning.

Jeepers Keepers

There are honourable exceptions in Ulster who have not lost the run of themselves. In July 2002, the *Sunday World* asked me to do player-profiles of everyone due to play in the All-Ireland quarter-finals. With eight teams involved, they wanted me to write pen-pictures of 120 players. That is a pretty difficult exercise. When you have to write about 16 corner-backs, it is very hard to find 16 different ways of saying 'tight-marker' and 'tenacious'.

My problems began, though, with the goalkeepers. There are not too many things you can say about a goalie other than he is a 'good shot-stopper', 'has great reflexes' and 'has a good kickout'. Generally the only variable is whether you can use 'very agile'. By the time I got to the last goalkeeper on the list, Armagh's Benny Tierney, I was getting very bored with repeating myself so I described him as 'fat and overweight'. He came up with a great retort: 'Spillane is right. Yes, I am fat and overweight now, but he will always be ugly.' I salute Benny for keeping a bit of humour in the game, and I just wish there were a few more like him up north.

The Memory Man

My fifth problem with Ulster football was personal. They all hate me up there! Jimmy Magee often relates the story from the days he was commentating on UTV, when he was walking across the pitch in Clones after an Ulster football Championship match and an Ulster football fan came up to him and said, 'Tell that b****x Spillane he knows nothing about football.' Jimmy replied, 'Hang on a minute. He has eight All-Ireland medals and nine All-Star awards. He must know something about football.' The fella walked away muttering obscenities and casting all kinds of aspersions about me and my parents.

One night I was the main speaker at a major function of a prominent club in Ulster. At the end of the night a spectator went up to the MC for the evening, Adrian Logan from UTV, and said, 'Twas shocking to hear all that filthy language here this evening. That kind of talk has no place in the GAA.'

Adrian nodded and just to make conversation asked the man what he thought of Pat Spillane. Logan was surprised with his response, 'I can't stand that f*****g c***. He only talks 'sh*t*.'

There's No Show Like a Joe Show

The sixth reason why I objected to Ulster football was that it had inflicted Joe Brolly on us! In the 1990s, Derry football produced one of the great characters in the history of the game, Brolly. He did things his way, like blowing kisses to fans after he scored a goal. This caused one Derry fan to remark: 'At the best of times Joe Brolly is objectionable, but when he blows kisses he's highly objectionable.'

Brolly never really surrendered to managers and was never short of self-confidence. This did not always endear him to his managers. One of them was heard to say, 'He's down there now letting people how good he is playing.'

Brolly wasn't always complimentary to his team-mates. After a club game, a disconsolate new recruit to the team said, 'I've never played so badly before.'

Brolly appeared surprised, 'You mean you've played before?'

After a county game, one of his colleagues said proudly, 'That was the best game I ever played'.

Brolly replied, 'Well you mustn't let that discourage you.'

Mea Culpa

Brolly is a good friend of mine, but sometimes he's away with the fairies, and often in the middle of an analysis of a match on the telly he, like myself, goes off on a tangent. During the Connacht semifinal between Mayo and Galway in 2004, as Colm O'Rourke was engaging in typically incisive analysis, Brolly butted in to describe pony-tailed Kieran McDonald: 'He looks like a Swedish maid.' As Michael Lyster tried to get serious again, Brolly decided to interject a comment about Mayo's Conor Mortimer: 'He would be better off spending more time practising his shooting and less in the hairdressers.'

While most people claim they never know what I'm going to say next, I haven't a clue in the world what Brolly is going to say. He can be very infuriating. I would have prepared my contribution and had what I thought was a great joke ready and might be just about to use it, when Brolly would butt in and say something nonsensical and burst out laughing, destroying my whole momentum. The opportunity to use my carefully crafted joke would be gone.

One of my few regrets about being an analyst goes back to 2003. The first round draw for the back door into the Leinster Championship was being made. After the discussion on the glamour games, we turned to a discussion on the so-called lesser lights. Brolly had long since lost interest and was getting very giddy. I was taking a great interest in what was going on and had a point to make about each match. On this occasion, though, Brolly's giddiness got to me and I got sucked into it as well. When we came to the last match, which involved Carlow, we were both giggling and seemed to be making a joke of it as if the match didn't matter. After the programme, a lot of comments came in about how flippant we were and the way we degraded Carlow football.

At the end of every year, I can normally stand over everything I have said on television, but this was one time I have to hold up my hands in the air and say Carlow football was treated with disrespect, but it was Brolly who was responsible. He dragged me down to his level. It was wrong of me to let him, and I must acknowledge that. Eagle-eyed viewers will have noted that Brolly and myself have not been paired together lately. RTÉ have recognised that it is a recipe for disaster.

To prove that Murphy's law is alive and well, in one of my first nights presenting *The Sunday Game* this year, after Meath beat Wicklow, I asked Bernard Flynn how well Meath would cope with Mick O'Dwyer's Laois in the Leinster semifinal. The only problem was that Laois hadn't even played the quarter-final against Carlow at that stage! Yet another apology due to the Carlow people.

The Last Supper

Brolly was responsible for one of the most painful evenings of my life. I make a lot of after-dinner speeches. One of my worst such experiences was up in Dungiven hurling club. If I was being well paid for it I wouldn't have minded, but I was doing it as a favour for Brolly.

I arrived late. Everyone was plastered. The 300-plus attendance was exclusively male. They were all in their monkey-suits, but there were a lot of earrings and a lot of tattoos. It was a very intimidating audience. I sat alongside the chief officer of the club who deeply resented that a football guy was there giving a speech. The former Offaly hurler Pat Delaney spoke before me. His speech was about patriotism, nationalism and how hurling was a 32-county sport. He extolled the joys of hurling and got an incredible response. I knew that I had all my gags ready and thought this was going to be a real belter. As they were lapping up Delaney's speech, I should have realised that the writing was on the wall. I started into my speech and two minutes later a guy stood up and said, 'We don't like what you say about Ulster football.' He was quickly told to shut up. I thought to myself that with my gags ready, I would be able to bring the crowd under control.

Five minutes later a different man got up and said, 'Feck you. We don't like what you say about Ulster football.' Thankfully one of my team-mates from the International Rules football team, Brian Gilligan, went down to him and told him to sit down. When big Brian tells you to sit down, you sit down.

One of the many incidents Brian is remembered for goes back to one of his appearances for Ireland in the Compromise Rules series against Australia. The teams were coming off the pitch and one of the Aussies was chastising the Cavan midfielder, Stephen King. Brian was coming up behind Stephen and wasn't very impressed with what he saw. He went up and knocked the Aussie's gum-shield out of his mouth and stamped on it with his foot. Nobody ever saw anybody shutting up so quickly. Thankfully Brian had the same effect in Dungiven.

I plodded on and spoke for a further 25 minutes. I died a death. At the end of the speech, the chairman got up and said, 'I'd just like to reiterate that the name of this club is not Dungiven hurling club. It's the Kevin Lynch hurling club.' With that the roof was nearly lifted off such was the round of applause he got. Who was Kevin Lynch? I did not know then but I certainly know now. He was one of the hunger strikers in 1981. To this day, I hold on to the black biro that was presented to me that night with 'Kevin Lynch, Dungiven', written on it. A reminder of one of my bad days.

The Life of Ryan

Before last Christmas, I attended a function in Bundoran, Co Donegal, for Dromore GAA club in Tyrone, Ryan McMenamin's club. They cleared over stg£80,000 in profit. Northern clubs have great ability to raise funds. It is not because they have wealthier members than down south, but because they can get people to dig deeper into their pockets for the sake of the club. I genuinely take my hat off to them for that.

One of the things they had at the function was an auction. The pattern in these GAA functions is always the same. There is always an auction with a hurley signed by DJ Carey. That night the auctioneer was Andrew Nesbitt, the Irish rally champion. It was a very ecumenical choice as Andrew is a Protestant from Portadown and was brought up in a culture a bit different from Dromore GAA club. Andrew is a lovely guy. At one stage as he was auctioning DJ's hurley, when he was on £1100, he turned to me and whispered, 'You know there's only one bidder. If they find out I'm in trouble.' Fair play to him he got it up to £1700. What I found interesting was that the proud new owner was Pat Doherty, the senior member of Sinn Féin, who bought it on behalf of the party. Nobody made any jokes about what he intended to use the hurley for.

Another item for auction were the boots Peter Canavan wore in the 2003 All-Ireland final. I've now been at five auctions where Peter's boots from that game were auctioned. Who knew he wore so many boots?

As the function was going so well, I asked for a Tyrone jersey and wrote: 'Sorry, I was wrong. Up Tyrone. Pat Spillane.' I threw off my coat, put the jersey on me, and stood on the table and somebody bought it for £2500.

When I go up north, they don't expect me to grovel. They know exactly what I'm like and they expect me to slag them off. It's funny that the more I slag them, the more often they invite me up and the more they pay me!

In 1994 I did a function in Tyrone, and earlier this year I returned to the same venue. My opening words of ten years ago were quoted back to me in full. Peter Canavan was in the audience in 1994, and I began by saying: 'I look down the hall and I see before me Peter Canavan, one of the greatest Tyrone players of all time. They call Peter Canavan "God" up here. They call me a b****x. I have eight All-Ireland medals and Peter Canavan has none.'

My Road to Damascus

Apart from the general dourness and lack of joy in their play, there were a number of specific incidents in the last two years that made me uneasy about Ulster football. There was the way the Armagh players lined up before the 2003 All-Ireland final. I will never forget the frightening intensity on their faces on what should have been the happiest day of a player's life. Likewise the previous year, the Armagh players received their All-Stars without a smile or a flicker of emotion as if smiling sent out a signal that they were satisfied. However, what I found most frustrating was watching Tyrone in 2003 and seeing them play so defensively when I knew the exciting brand of football they were capable of. It was so disappointing to see them play a type of game that was alien to them the year before. In fairness, I must concede that even the great Kerry team was happy to win an All-Ireland playing ugly rather than lose it playing pretty.

This is not the place for a treatise of how the GAA in the north has been affected by the Troubles, but I always try to understand their situation where for years playing football was a dangerous activity given the political climate. As an analyst, I am always aware that when I critisise an Ulster footballer, given the depth of feeling about the game there, I am seen as also criticising their club, county and province. You have to give them credit. Ulster fans are the most passionate in the game.

This is not a frantic attempt to get myself back in their good books, but this year I have come to realise that we have a lot of reasons to be grateful to the Ulster counties, principally because they raised the bar in terms of preparation, sacrifices and commitment and it is up to the other counties to follow. This year they have followed. What the Ulster counties forgot was that the southern boys were quick learners. Yet the best performance in 2004 by far was Armagh's defeat of Donegal in the Ulster final. The second best was probably Armagh's defeat of Monaghan – even allowing for Monaghan's limitations. In recent years the best Championship football has generally been played in Ulster. Although it was Kerry and Mayo who contested the All-Ireland final, if we were to rank the top six footballing counties this year, four of them would be from Ulster. They haven't gone away you know! Ulster football is still the tops. They have reaped what they have sowed. They put more into it than anybody else and they got their rewards in 2002 and 2003. They will get them again in the coming years.

I have to confess, though, that the team who have most changed my attitude to Ulster football is Fermanagh. They have 'erned' my undying gratitude for bringing the joy innocence and fun back to football. They brought simplicity and new life into a Championship that might otherwise have fallen into the categories of dull, boring and overcomplicated. Lads, I salute ye.

The Last Laugh

Invariably the Ulster fans have their own revenge on me. They call me 'the funeral director' because they claim that I am always miserable looking. They also say: 'Remember the good old days when the only thing that annoyed you about television was poor reception. Now the reception is perfect, but they have sent Pat Spillane to punish us instead.' They also had a Pat Spillane anagram competition. Apparently the best anagram is Pet Anal Lips.

In Armagh they still go on about my infamous comments at half-time in the 2002 All-Ireland final, especially about my mother's arthritis.

In retaliation they have a story about a conversation that they say took place between my mother and me when I was eight.

'Mam! I think I've been selected for the school Gaelic team.'

'That's good,' replied my mother, 'but why aren't you sure?'

'Well, it hasn't been announced officially, but I overheard the coach saying that if I were in the team I'd be a great drawback.'

I am reliably informed, though, that the most popular joke going around the province involves me walking into a sperm donor bank and saying to the receptionist, 'I'd like to donate some sperm.'

'Have you ever donated before?' she asked.

'Yes,' I replied, 'you should have my details on your computer.'

'Oh yes,' said the receptionist, 'but I see you're going to need help. Shall I get a lap dancer for you?'

'Why do I need help?' I asked.

The receptionist replied, 'Well, it said on your record that you're a useless w*****.'

6

Parting is Such Sorrow

We live in a strange world which, at times, is very difficult to understand. We have a habit of getting our priorities all wrong. The most famous saying in the sporting vernacular is Bill Shankly's oft-quoted dictum that: 'Football is not a matter of life and death. It is much more important.'

Treating sport as a life-and-death issue is a classic example of what I'm talking about. Far too many of us spend too much time complaining about small things and overlooking the big picture. Every day we experience a complex set of emotions which can make us happy, sad and frustrated, all within a short space of time. But above everything else, we live in a world where there are so many unanswered questions.

All these thoughts struck me the first Tuesday morning in March 2004, when I heard the shocking news that Cormac McAnallen had died. For once in my life I was stuck for words.

Why would God take such a gifted role model? Cormac was a superb sportsman, a gentleman to his finger tips and somebody who had contributed so much, both on and off the field, during his 24 years of life. Why leave all the bad people and take one of the good guys? Sorry, God, but there are times when this religion lark completely fails me. Over the years I have listened to priests at funeral masses trying to explain why good guys have been taken away in the prime of their lives. But I have yet to hear a satisfactory answer.

Cormac McAnallen was an icon of modern-day Gaelic football. A tremendous athlete, he was blessed with a great engine. He was an outstanding fielder and a versatile performer. But it was another quality which meant he stood out from all his colleagues. He was blessed with a maturity that stretched way beyond his tender years. It was no surprise when Mickey Harte chose him to captain Tyrone in 2004.

In his tragically short time on earth, Cormac achieved more than most will ever manage in a lifetime. He captained Tyrone to victory in the All-Ireland minor and U-21 Championships; he won an All-Ireland senior medal; he is a former Young Player of the Year and an All-Star; and he represented Ireland with distinction in the 2003 Compromise Rule series. And they are just the high points.

I have heard many compelling arguments as to the reasons why Tyrone finally reached football's promised land in 2003. There was the deployment of their brilliant two-man full-forward line, their use of the blanket defence and Brian Dooher's role as a link-man. I believe, however, that Tyrone's trump card was Cormac McAnallen's performances at full-back. The decision of Mickey Harte to switch the star midfielder to the edge of the square after the team leaked four goals in the drawn Ulster final was the final piece of the jigsaw. From that moment on, Tyrone never looked back. While nothing is ever certain in football, I think it's safe to predict that Cormac would have won more than one Celtic Cross.

Cormac produced his fair share, way more than his fair share, of memorable victories and epic performances, which have ignited the imagination of Gaelic football fans. The craft and courage of this young man has added another marvellous chapter to the already richly garlanded history of a sport that demands skill, speed, strength and character. The fervent hope is that others can emulate his lofty standards. If young players in the future can live up to his trademark determination and staggering dignity, it will be a magnificent legacy he has left to us.

Cormac was a hero in the true sense of the term, because when he performed well, *do luigh an laoch san uile dhuine* (the hero in all of us was exulted). From the dawn of time, identification with heroes has been an integral part of the human condition. Great sporting performances have always grabbed the imagination of the young of all ages as they fantasise about emulating the glorious feats of their heroes. Thanks in no small part to television, sports heroes occupy an even larger part of the imagination than in earlier generations. The realisation that we had lost Cormac forever generated a sense of loss which far exceeded anything that would have been felt for any politician or media personality. Even the most casual of fans took vicarious pride in the style, craft, courage and character of this young man.

Cormac's presence will linger with us forever. As John O'Donohue wrote in *Eternal Echoes*:

> *Memory rescues experience from total disappearance ... the grooves in the mind hold traces and vestiges of everything that has ever happened to us. Nothing is ever lost or forgotten ... a ruin is never simply empty. It remains a vivid temple of absence.*

I was numb when I heard the news of Cormac's death. I didn't know him personally, but I feel I have lost a valued member of my extended family, the GAA. For what its worth, my heart goes out to his parents, Brendan and Bridget, his brothers, Donal and Fergus, his fiancée, Aisling, his team-mates at club and county level, and to the people of Tyrone.

The late American sports writer, Grantland Rice, wrote: 'For when the great scorer comes to write against your name, He makes not how you won or lost, but how you played the game.' Cormac McAnallen personified this.

Nobody did more than Cormac McAnallen to make the sport I love so well the beautiful game.

Ar dheis Dé go raibh a anam.

7

The Top 10 GAA Computer Viruses

The Government Department of Information and Technology has issued an urgent alert to all computer owners to be on the lookout for a number of nasty viruses that are currently threatening computer software throughout the country. Be vigilant for the following 'GAA computer viruses' and the symptoms which identify them.

1. **The Ulster Football Virus**
   People have been known to get sick just looking at it.

2. **The Páidí Ó Sé Virus**
   Difficult to get rid of, will not go off screen.

3. **The Liam Griffin Virus**
   Keeps repeating, 'Hurling is the Riverdance of sport.'

4. **The Ex-GAA Presidents Virus**
   Only allows you to print copies of *Harry Potter and the Chamber Of Secrets*.

5. **The Tommy Lyons Virus**
   Only allows your system to function one year
   in every three.

6. **The Meath Football Virus**
   Likely to throw you out of Windows.

7. **The Pat Spillane Golden Era Virus**

   Only responds to dates between 1975 and 1986.

8. **The Traditionalist Virus**

   Insists on constantly replaying the old theme music to *The Sunday Game*.

9. **The Shane Curran Virus**

   You can never predict what will happen next.

10. **The Seán Boylan Virus**

    Goes on forever.

8

All the President's Men

I admit it. I get angry often. I know some people think I am also
arrogant because I air my views so trenchantly. To highlight this,
the story is told about the day I faced God at the throne of heaven
with Colm O'Rourke and Joe Brolly. God said to us, 'Before
granting you a place at my side, I must ask for your beliefs.'

Brolly stared God directly in the eye and said, 'I believe Gaelic
football is the meaning of life. Nothing else has brought so much
joy to so many. I have devoted my life to spreading the gospel of
football.'

God was moved by his passion and eloquence and said, 'You
are a man of true faith. Sit by me at my right hand.' He then
turned to Meath's most famous son, 'Now, my child, tell me
what you believe in?'

'I believe that courage, bravery, loyalty, team-work, dedication
and commitment are the soul of life, and I dedicated my career to
living up to those ideals.'

God replied, 'You have spoken well my child. Sit by me at my
left hand.'

He then turned to me, 'And you, Mr Spillane, what is it that
you believe?'

I gave him the withering look that I usually reserve for those
who engage in puke football and replied, 'I believe that you are
sitting in my chair.'

In actual fact, though, I am acutely aware that GAA analysts
are not to be taken too seriously. Hence I enjoy the story of the

traveller wandering on an island inhabited entirely by cannibals. He comes upon a butcher's shop, which specialises in human brains. The human brains are differentiated by source. A sign in the shop reads: 'Scientists' brains €20 per lb, economists' brains €40 per lb, philosophers' brains €60 per lb and GAA analysts' brains €2000 per lb.' The traveller asks how it is that GAA analysts' brains are so expensive. The butcher says: 'It's because you have to kill 100 times more GAA analysts to get a pound of brains.'

Several years ago, after the success of *The Premiership*, the editors and the directors in charge of *The Sunday Game* wanted to jazz it up and make it punchier. They suggested to Colm O'Rourke and I that we should ape what Johnny Giles and Eamon Dunphy did. Why can't one be thoughtful and analytical *à la* Giles and one a bit of a loose canon and controversial *à la* Dunphy? In rare moments of vanity I'm very pleased to think that in recent years I have lived up to their instructions. I think I have done a great job in the Giles role!

It has been said that when it comes to GAA punditry, there are three kinds of fools – the pundits themselves, the newspaper editors and TV producers who hire them, and above all, the people who read or listen to them. I know that I annoy a lot of people and am quite happy to be slagged off or to be the butt of comments like, 'What is the biggest joke I know? Pat Spillane,' or alternatively, 'We have the problem of spam on the Internet and the problem of Spillane on TV.' I think the definitive one is about me and Quasimodo.

Quasimodo is sat in his study and once again is feeling depressed about how ugly he is. Looking for some reassurance, he goes in search of Esmeralda. When he finds her, he asks her again if he really is the ugliest man alive.

Esmeralda sighs and she says, 'Look, why don't you go upstairs and ask the magic mirror who is the ugliest man alive. The mirror will answer your question once and for all.'

About five minutes later, a very pleased looking Quasimodo bounced back the stairs and gave Esmeralda a great big hug.

'Well it worked,' Quasimodo beamed, 'but who on earth is Pat Spillane?'

I enjoy a good joke as much as anybody, even when it's against me, but there are some issues that really get me worked up.

Open Sesame?

In my 40-year involvement with the GAA, I have never felt as ashamed as I did last March when news broke that there would be no debate on Rule 42, about opening up Croke Park, at Congress. That was the week that Brazilian World Cup star Gerson was so disgusted at being omitted from Pele's list of top 125 footballers that he tore up the list live on television. I felt like doing the same with my GAA membership card. The GAA's Motions Committee, which consists of ex-GAA Presidents, decreed that none of the motions pertaining to Rule 42 should be debated as they were 'out of order' on technical grounds. Who are this unelected elite group to defy the wishes of the majority of GAA members? How dare they deny their fellow members the chance to air their views on this important topic on the floor of Congress. How dare a group, who are effectively has-beens who were handed their P45s long ago, still have such a major say in the running of the organisation.

Their decision smacks of the worst excesses of dictatorship. They behave like an ageing politburo, determined to hold on to the strings of the power – and occasionally they manage to do just that. As an organisation, the GAA prides itself on its democracy. The reality couldn't be further from the truth. The GAA's version of democracy is a bit like the one George Orwell wrote about in *Animal Farm*: 'All animals are equal, but some animals are more equal than others.'

The decision is yet another nail in the coffin of the GAA's flawed version of democracy. The bottom line is that the motions to amend Rule 42, which I believe would have had the support of a majority of Association members, did not get an airing at Congress in Killarney in April 2004. Why? Because these elder lemons found some technical flaws in the motions and opted not to correct those minor flaws, even though they were well within their rights to do so. The decision wouldn't have been out of place in Ceausescu's Romania.

In 2003, Éire Óg delegate Pat Daly said at the GAA Convention in Cork: 'It's about time the GAA woke up. The ban has been gone since 1973 – if Frank Sinatra can play in Croke Park, then why not the Irish international rugby team?' However, Munster Council Treasurer Dan Hoare went for an 'out, out, out' approach: 'I would not let anybody into the car park, not to mention into Croke Park.' That is the kind of 'no surrender' attitude that Ian Paisley would be proud of. Last year a delegate at the Wicklow GAA County Convention said: 'We are being asked to wake up some morning and see the English soccer team playing in Croke Park. Just 80 years ago the English came to Croke Park and shot Gaelic players.'

The big hitters in the association had been lining up behind the 'No' campaign from early in the year. And boy did they come out firing on all cylinders. Ex-GAA President Jack Boothman was the first to join battle. He sent a letter to selected elected officers pleading with them not to change the rule. This is the second time in three years that Jack has played that particular card. Unfortunately it has had the desired impact on both occasions.

Ulster Says No

The usual suspects from Ulster then came out of the woodwork. Of course, we should not have been in the least surprised that the Ulster counties are so trenchant in their support of Rule 42. Council Secretary Danny Murphy suggested that unless there was a clear case for change, then there were definite reasons not to change. Work out that logic if you can. If you do, you are way smarter than I am.

Newly-elected Ulster Council President Michael Greenan weighed in with a real beauty. He said the GAA were not in the business of housing the homeless. So much for the age-old proverb that we teach our children that sharing is caring. I suppose we should not be surprised at the degree of narrow-mindedness emanating from this source. After all, this was the same Council that dug its heels in and insisted that a provincial semifinal between Donegal and Derry be played on the same afternoon that the Republic of Ireland played Spain in a World Cup soccer match in 2002. So long as units of the GAA make those kind of preposterous decisions, opponents of the Association are never short of ammunition to fire at Croke Park.

To stress the small-mindedness of the Ulster Council on the day of the Ireland–Spain match, a journalist brought a portable television into the press box to keep an eye on the Ireland game. When he was spotted, he was promptly and pompously told by an official that it was not appropriate to have a TV there for that purpose and that he must turn it off.

What I find most difficult is that the Ulster Council, who espouse such lofty principles and are such great champions of tradition, could then do a 'Jerry Maguire' on it and say 'Show me the money,' and have the Ulster final played in Croke Park. Lofty principles are great, but one of the hypocrisies of the GAA world is that when money comes into it, tradition and ideals go out the window.

Many of these former GAA bureaucrats have one great weapon which they use with consummate skill – the GAA rule book. They are greatly helped by the rule book, which is badly constructed and written in such a way that those of us who didn't get grinds in GAA-speak would find it easier to read cave writings from the Stone Age. Of course if, by some miracle, a rule is capable of producing a measure which will drag the organisation kicking and screaming into the twenty-first century, the old guard have yet another weapon in their arsenal – a technicality. What is even more galling for me is that, in blocking progress in this way, they say in all earnestness that they are acting in 'the best interests of the GAA'.

Can you believe this kind of thing is still going on? Surely as the foremost sporting organisation in Ireland, our role is to provide youngsters with as many sporting opportunities as possible, rather than having them messing up their lives with drugs or whatever. Opening up Croke Park would present new possibilities to fund much-needed coaching initiatives for the next generation of footballers and hurlers.

Kelly's Anti-heroes

The person I felt most sympathy for in all this mess was current GAA president Seán Kelly. To quote Britney Spears: 'Oops I did it again'. I have now offended many officers in the GAA yet again by not describing Seán as 'Uachtarán Cumann Lúthchleas Gael'.

> *Admhaím do Dhia uilechumhachtach*
> *agus duoibhse, a bhráithre,*
> *gur pheacaigh mé go trom.*
> *A Thiarna, déan trócaire.*

If you didn't understand those last four lines, you have no chance of ever rising to even lowly office in the GAA. Those of you who did will recognise it as a prayer asking for forgiveness and mercy. Sadly given my propensity to put my foot in my mouth, this is the prayer I have to say the most often!

Seán Kelly's views on the Croke Park issue are well known. Unlike the dinosaurs who disallowed all the motions, he is a man with his finger on the pulse of how the association is thinking on this issue. He knows that the majority of members want to amend Rule 42. But his predecessors, who should no longer have any role in the running of the Association, have left him hanging out to dry. Cork County Board had a real go at him. They are the most powerful County Board in the county and can use or abuse this power as they see fit. I saw this a few years ago at first hand.

A high-powered committee including the likes of Colm O'Rourke and Martin Carney was set up to look into Gaelic football, and one of their suggestions was that the National League should be scrapped. I felt this was wrong because the more competitions you have and the more high-profile games you have, the better. I wrote an article on that theme in the *Sunday World*, strongly criticising the proposal. The morning the article appeared, I got a call from an officer of the Cork County Board. Obviously I was aware of which official on the Cork County Board had prompted this officer to ring me. I was asked if I would like more material in relation to the proposal, which would outline why it was so undesirable. Later that afternoon, 10 pages were faxed through from the Cork County Board. It was like manna from heaven for a lazy journalist because I was able to get three further articles out of it for my column in the *Sunday World*. What really brought home to me just how powerful the Cork County Board are, was that the week before the vote was taken on the Committee's proposal at Congress, that particular officer was able to tell me the exact outcome of the vote.

Hard Times

The Rule 42 debacle last March was a black and bleak time for the GAA. Members were denied freedom of speech, as a group of ex-Presidents effectively decided that the Association's central Council couldn't be trusted on such a fundamental policy issue as opening up Croke Park. Of course, the GAA also lost the opportunity to earn much-needed cash from renting Croke Park out to the FAI and the IRFU. The actions of a few have resulted in the GAA's scoring one of the biggest own goals since the infamous RDS affair.

Having read my column on the Rule 42 shambles in the *Sunday World,* a number of people urged me to make some form of protest against the decision of the ex-GAA presidents to rule out all the motions relating to Croke Park. Outspoken though I am on many GAA topics, unfortunately – or maybe that should read fortunately – I'm not a modern-day Jim Larkin. I know from previous experience that trying to talk sense to some of the head chiefs in the GAA is akin to beating your head against a stone wall.

Several commentators at the time, including Colm O'Rourke and my *Sunday World* colleague Roy Curtis, suggested that the whole fiasco ought to be a resigning issue for GAA president, Seán Kelly. Although the former presidents hung him out to dry, and then he was further humiliated by being forced to defend and explain the actions of the Committee, I disagreed. Resigning was not an option. It would not have solved anything. Instead, it would simply be giving in to those pampered out-of-touch individuals.

Some of the rhetoric which poured forth from the pro-Rule 42 brigade in March 2004 when the controversy was at its height made my blood boil. As a GAA member, I felt ashamed when I heard some of the arguments. In particular, the *Prime Time* debate on the subject was cringeworthy. The Cork representative who appeared on the programme was stuck in a time warp of outdated patriotism. He argued that the GAA should keep the ban in place as a result of what happened in Croke Park on Bloody Sunday.

It is very sad to see people living in the past. If everybody was dwelling on what happened decades ago, we would never have had the Peace Process and we would be still waking up every morning as we used to in the 1970s and 1980s to hear headlines like: 'A part-time member of the UDR has been murdered by the IRA in County Tyrone.' Or we would be hearing about a poor Catholic who had been savagely murdered by a Loyalist organisation. The logic of those still living in the past is that Irish people shouldn't eat Danish bacon or drink Carlsberg because of what the Danes did to poor Brian Boru at Clontarf in 1014!

One can argue until the cows come home about the GAA's rule book. It is a bit like having a debate about religion and taking selected passages from the Bible to justify any argument. Even if the GAA Presidents were technically correct in their ruling, what about Rule 74, which states that Congress should take precedent? Or what about Rule 4, which states that the GAA should support Irish business? They won't be doing much for Irish business if thousands of Irish fans are forced to travel to Britain for Ireland's home games in soccer and rugby when Lansdowne Road is closed for renovations.

What I also found revealing was that at a meeting of Central Council, rather than trying to learn a lesson from the debacle, delegates had expressed annoyance at the manner in which ex-presidents had been 'pilloried' for their decision to declare the motions relating to Rule 42 out of order. Down's Dan McCartan said it was disturbing that men who had served the GAA so well were subjected to severe personal attacks: 'It is deplorable that they should be treated so badly by our own members. Those who made the attacks brought shame on the Association.'

Yet again I have brought shame on the GAA. For more years than I care to remember, senior GAA figures have pressurised RTÉ to get rid of me from *The Sunday Game* programme. Thankfully, the crusade has failed. There are many within the association who regard me as an anti-GAA figure, willing to do anything to damage the reputation of the Association. Nothing could be further from the truth. Just to emphasise how unfounded their argument is, let me detail my 'GAA schedule' for the weekend in March 2004 when I wrote my angriest column ever about GAA officialdom. I spent Saturday morning cleaning the Templenoe GAA club dressing-rooms. In the afternoon I attended an Under-16 club match, while later that night I spent time collecting membership fees. On Sunday morning, I refereed two juvenile matches before tuning in to TG4's coverage of the Kerry–Westmeath League tie. A radical and a trouble-maker for the GAA? I don't think so.

Shooting the messenger has been a national pastime in Ireland for as long as I can remember. Many within the GAA hierarchy have taken it to a fine art. Badger baiting and cock fighting were also national pastimes, but they have been outlawed. Hopefully shooting the messenger will suffer a similar fate.

Cork's Bob Honohan has suggested, though, that it was the former presidents who were in touch with the real ethos of the association. On the Saturday evening of Congress as the delegates were sitting down to a lavish banquet in Killarney, I was in Killarney as well.

I told my family I would like to go to Congress this year. My wife told me though that I would need a bodyguard as the delegates would kill me because of all the things I had said down the years. My brothers told her that she must be joking. I would need at least ten bodyguards. We never got to that situation as for some mysterious reason I never got an invitation. There must have been a problem with the post. So that same April evening, I was getting cold and wet in Killarney while acting as a linesman at a Division 5 Kerry League game between Templenoe and Dr Crokes B. Might I respectfully suggest that I'm more in touch with the GAA's real ethos than the ex-Presidents.

Unfortunately there are many narrow-minded GAA members who are stuck in a time warp. They are holding the majority to ransom and giving two fingers to democracy and free speech. May I suggest that these ageing dinosaurs be thanked for their past contribution and then gracefully retired.

At Congress, Seán Kelly summed up my own feelings on this issue when he suggested to delegates that when knowledge of the rules is the preserve of the few, there is a risk of this small cabal exerting too much power. This is surely the case at the moment. I cannot understand the hypocrisy and inconsistency which prevails amongst these gentlemen. They vetoed all eight motions on Rule 42, yet they had the power to correct them and allow them to go before Congress. At the same time, they allowed another motion, relating to what competitions under-age players are allowed to participate in, even though it was universally accepted that there were major technical flaws in it.

It is interesting in this context that when Ireland played Nigeria at Charlton Athletic's ground in London in June, the Irish team was delayed from getting on the pitch for their warm-up because a Gaelic football match was going on. How would we react if the FA brought in a rule to forbid Gaelic football from being played on soccer pitches? I have been friendly with Brian Kerr for many years. During his days as manager of St Pat's, Brian heard that representatives from Dynamo Bucharest were watching a training session before a European tie. To ensure that the opposition were as bemused as possible, he instructed his players to play a Gaelic football match for the entire session! If other sports can be so ecumenical, why can't we?

The GAA is so concerned with protecting our 'cultural purity', yet it has been more than willing to take the shilling when those well-known champions of Irish culture Sir Elton O'Seán, Billy O'Joel agus Neil O'Diamond have sold their wares in Croke Park. Even more amazingly, the GAA was happy to host an American football match there in 1997. Does that seem consistent to you?

Of the People, for the People, by the People?

The GAA delegates in Cork didn't want Brian O'Driscoll or Damien Duff to grace Croke Park. Yet they were happy to have that well-known role model for young children, Michael Jackson, on the sacred sod in their own stadium in Cork. The whole thing is definitely not a 'Thriller'. In fact it's 'Bad'.

In arguing for the opening of Croke Park, I have little interest in bailing out our sporting brothers in the FAI or the IRFU for their ineptitude and shortcomings over the last 40 years. My plea is born out of economic necessity. The GAA needs to capitalise on its biggest asset and to use the money earned to develop Gaelic games, particularly at youth level. Sadly, the debate so far has seen fellows emerge out of the woodwork whose mind-set is stuck firmly in the nineteenth century.

Motions to amend Rule 42 were allowed to go before Congress in 2001 and 2002, so why were similar proposals out of order in 2004?

The Chief Executive of the Gaelic Players' Association (GPA), Dessie Farrell, got to the nub of the issue: 'This is a blatant and dictatorial departure from anything resembling democracy and one would have to question the structures and procedures that have ultimately delivered the body blow to the GAA's membership. This issue warrants a full and democratic hearing at the top table. However, the question must now be asked just where the top actually resides. Is it within the supposedly hallowed, but arguably flawed, democracy of Congress, or amongst a gathering of former presidents under the innocuous banner of the Motions Committee? The average GAA person has never been as far removed from the decision-making process and we would urge all units and members of the Association to persevere with the difficult questions that need answering at this time.'

The GAA is not an organisation based on democracy but on a democratic deficit. It likes to pretend the ordinary club member has as much say in its running as the highest-ranking office holder. The reality is very different from the rhetoric. Try getting any kind of innovative or controversial motion on to the floor of Congress and you'll see what I mean. Every obstacle is placed in the way to frustrate your efforts.

One of the media's annual rituals every Christmas is to publish the sports quotes of the year. Former Wexford hurling manager Liam Griffin stole the honours in 2000 with his comments on the GAA, 'I have never seen an organisation so hidebound by bulls**t.' The Rule 42 fiasco underlines the truth of his words.

The historian Barbara Tuchman has pointed out that empires and institutions have a way of hastening their own destruction by arrogant decisions, which are entirely self-defeating. Instead of listening to sincere cries for meaningful reform, they have attempted to impose their authority in high-handed fashion. It sounds like she was basing her research on the GAA.

Changing Times

In many ways, though, I would compare the plight of the GAA today with that of the Catholic Church. My family have played a modest role in Irish sporting history, but we were also peripherally involved in one of Ireland's greatest religious occasions. Early in 1979, news broke that the Pope would visit Ireland that September. The Pope's visit touched something very deep in the Irish psyche. It was like three Christmases rolled into one. Even the most sceptical were caught up in the occasion. As thousands of pilgrims waited on Galway racecourse on a misty September Sunday morning, they laughed heartily at Bishop Eamonn Casey and Fr Michael Cleary's warm-up performance, a roller-coaster of fun and frolics.

My mother is a devout Catholic so when Pope John Paul II came to Ireland, it was a major event for the family. My brother Mick presented an oak sapling to the Pope in Galway during the Papal Mass for the youth of Ireland, as part of the giving of gifts. It was an honour much cherished by all of us, and with the passing of the years it has grown in significance for the family.

However, think of all the changes that have taken place in the Catholic Church in Ireland since 1979. To take just one small example, think of the different perspectives people have of both Eamonn Casey and Michael Cleary today.

Radio Daze

Months on I still find the whole episode about Rule 42 stomach turning. Particularly since, at the end of September, the government made a magnificent gesture in donating 40 million euro for the completion of Croke Park. When people like those ex-GAA Presidents get together in a room, it's incredible the decisions that come out of it. Really you have to wonder if the grassroots feelings are being represented by them. I doubt it. I'd say the vast majority of GAA fans would be appalled by the issue. The crux of the problem is that the minority are not prepared to listen to the majority. It smacks of the tail wagging the dog.

This raises a bigger issue than just the use of Croke Park. Does the ordinary GAA member, the backbone and heartbeat of the organisation, have any relevance in the decision-making process anymore? The experience of Rule 42 would suggest that this is far from the case.

I have never felt so ANGRY about ANY topic. That battle was lost but I, for one, will continue the war.

9

GAA Congress Etiquette

The most important social event in the GAA calendar is the Annual Congress. Ostensibly, Congress is a forum for the GAA's democratic procedures to be used to advance the Association. If you believe that, you still believe in the tooth fairy! Its real function is to allow those with ambitions for high office in the GAA to network with the movers and shakers and to be heard to say the right things.

The following is a survivor's guide to successfully negotiating Congress, while keeping your prospects for upward mobility within the GAA still intact.

1. Clothes

Things you should wear

Your dress code should be a round-neck jumper.

Things you shouldn't wear

Definitely no micro-minis or leather gear.

2. Jewellery

Do wear a *fáinne*, a pioneer pin and maybe an Easter Lily. Maybe not.

Do not wear large crucifixes or chains.

3. Language

Speak Irish. Use words and phrases like *Uachtarán, clár, Cumann Lúthcleas Gael, Go raibh míle maith agat, i lár na páirce, iris oifigiúil*. Don't use American or, worse still, English slang.

4. Linguistic Protocol

Do say:

'Ulster says no.'

'Ex-presidents of the GAA still have a role to play.'

'Spillane is a boll*x.' (preferably say it in Irish)

Under no circumstances say:

'Hope Rule 42 gets on the *clár*.'

'Spillane talks a lot of sense.'

'Great to see Roy Keane back.'

5. Appropriate Discussion Topics

Do raise that old chestnut:

'We must promote hurling in the weaker counties.'

Don't ask:

'Do you think that David Beckham really bedded Rebecca Loos that time?'

6. Beware of Local Sensitivities

All congresses are essentially the same: a diet of pious platitudes, back-slapping in public, back-biting in private and jockeying for position. However, each has its own distinctive hue, depending on the location and what the media is complaining about at the time.

The golden rule is to never, ever, ever try to be smart or witty. Three rising stars in the GAA saw their presidential hopes in the future dashed for good by loose remarks at the Congress in Killarney earlier this year.

What they said:

'I haven't seen any of Páidí's "f***ing animals" around the place. Have you?'

'I don't suppose anybody around here still has their *Kerry for the Five-in-a-row* tee-shirts from 1982.'

'Would ye not be embarrassed by Jackie Healy-Rae down here?'

What they should have said:

'God, 'twas a disgrace Mick O'Dwyer didn't get the Irish job.'

'Seamus Darby definitely pushed Tommy Doyle in the back in 1982. If Jimmy Deenihan was in there he wouldn't have let it happen.'

'I never realised Kerry was the eighth wonder of the world.'

10

An Open Letter to Danny Lynch

Dear Danny,

I hope all is well with you and trust that you are looking forward to Christmas. May I be the first to wish you and all in Headquarters peace, happiness and festive greetings.

Speaking of the season of goodwill, I was still basking in the glow of a Kerry yuletide when I opened *The Examiner* on 7 January last and read the headline: 'Lynch accuses Spillane of "shooting from the lip".' The opening sentence set the tone for the article: 'A senior GAA official has condemned TV pundit Pat Spillane for recent criticisms of the Association.' The article went on explain that, 'Spillane was enraged the GAA did not do more to entice Setanta Ó hAilpín away from a career in Australian Rules last December. He also slammed Croke Park bosses for failing to utilise the talents of former players in building their games at grassroots level.'

After accusing me of 'shooting from the lip', rather than 'having any real basis' to my arguments, you went on to say: 'Contrary to Spillane's suggestion that the mindset of those involved at the top of the Association needs to be changed, I would remind him that the GAA has come an awful long way in the last 20 years and will continue to do things their way and will not be dictated to by anyone.'

I have to confess I felt really, really bad all that afternoon and evening. I had a yoghurt for my lunch. After I had eaten it, I discovered that the expiry date on it had passed three months earlier.

I thought that your broadside in 'the paper' would be the end to the Setanta saga, but no. You then wrote to *The Sunday World* saying: 'I never realised that Pat Spillane is so sensitive. Or is he a little like 'Murphy's Dog' – he can give it but can't take it? To show that there are no hard feelings, I would like to assure him that we're all aware of his self-proclaimed infallibility, even if he is wrong to imply that my meagre salary may be superior to his four main earners.'

I have to confess that news of my infallibility came as a welcome surprise to me. I seriously wish my remuneration was as lucrative as you appear to think. I was reminded of the gap between my aspirations for riches and the reality when I attended my daughter's parent-teacher meeting last week. When the teacher asked her what she wanted to be when she grew up, my daughter replied that she wanted to be a football pundit.

The teacher asked, 'Why have you chosen this career?'

'I dream of making a fortune from working on RTÉ, like my father,' she replied.

'Your father makes a fortune from working on RTÉ?' echoed the impressed teacher.

'No,' replied my little girl, 'but he always dreams of it.'

The only worse thing than being talked about is not being talked about. While I am obviously flattered that the GAA's PRO is so interested in what I have to say and that you appear to follow my comments so closely, I wonder if you could use your or the GAA's time a little more productively. Anyway that's a separate issue. I know you are sensitive to my suggestions so I won't presume to tell you how to do your job.

I write, though, to let you know the reasons for my 'criticisms of the association'. Let me first assure you that it is not that I want to ask you, in the words of Elvis Presley, to 'Love Me Tender'. My purpose is to raise questions and to offer opinions but not to 'dictate' anything. To paraphrase Groucho Marx I wouldn't like to belong to any organisation that would have me as a dictator. When I do criticise the GAA on precise points, my criticism is never prompted by cynicism, never global, but always trying to hit a very definite point with a definite purpose. My questions are a pastoral service, an effort to bridge the gap between what ordinary GAA fans are thinking and what the GAA bureaucrats are doing, while at the same time remaining very deeply concerned for the authenticity and identity of the organisation that has dominated my life. Are our present structures and practices the best they could be? Can they be made better and how? These are the questions that preoccupy me, Danny.

These are serious times. I think that at the moment the GAA needs serious people asking serious questions if we are to meet the serious challenges that confront us in the years ahead. Please don't see me as the enemy, Danny. I am not here to annoy you, but rather in my own way am trying to further the good of Gaelic football. It is not because I don't care that I am vocal in criticism, Danny, it is because I do care. When my long-suffering wife hears me singing, very badly, in the shower, 'God only knows what I'd be without you!', she knows I'm singing about the GAA and not about her.

Just to assuage any concerns you may have, Danny, I did not lose any sleep over your comments. Given the amount of hate mail I have received and the viciousness of much of it in the last 13 years for my remarks as a pundit, your 'shooting from the lip' comment did not cause me to even bat an eyelid. What did concern me though was your remark that yours truly had 'no real basis to his arguments'. Trying to give well-meaning advice to the GAA is like eating chocolate. You know it's not good for you, but you go on eating it anyway. So to let you know that I do have a basis for my argument, I am writing to you in an attempt to clear the air.

The GAA is facing its biggest ever crisis. Unless it is addressed, the Association could find itself in third place behind rugby and soccer in the pecking order of Irish sport within a generation. I know that prediction sounds alarmist. Believe me, however, I'm not just scaremongering. The crisis has nothing to do with the chronic state of Gaelic football or the gap between the best and the rest in hurling or even with the Croke Park debacle. Please excuse me at this point for going off on a tangent, Danny, but last March you suggested that there would be little in the way of negative fall-out from the decision not to allow Rule 42 to be even discussed in Congress. Yeah, and the captain of the *Titanic* used similar logic when he said the iceberg had only caused a small hole in the side of his ship!

Quite simply, the GAA is losing the battle to attract the country's youngsters to its organisation. The days when the GAA was the undisputed number one sports organisation for everybody from eight to 18 are long gone. At best, the conveyor belt is stumbling along. Believe me, the doomsday scenario of the GAA's stadia turning into white elephants because they don't have enough players to play their games is not as far fetched as it sounds. The GAA has already lost the battle in the country's major cities and many of the large towns. In urban Ireland, soccer is the number one sport among the male population, with rugby also making significant inroads into the GAA's base.

There are particular difficulties once youngsters reach the age of 16. By then many of them are working part-time in order to finance their weekend social activities which, in many cases, revolve around drinking. Very few are prepared to forfeit the chance of earning a few bob in order to concentrate on playing football or hurling. Let's face it, for some, playing Gaelic games would interrupt their drinking. It is interesting in this context to see that the GAA, who are so doctrinaire on issues like Croke Park, are happy to have the All-Ireland hurling Championship sponsored by a drinks company. But I digress.

Even in GAA strongholds, youngsters are not playing Gaelic games. Take, for example, the school in Bantry where I teach, whose hinterland is a traditional area for Gaelic games among the bulk of Irish youngsters. The majority of Irish teenagers would, I venture to suggest, find it difficult to identify even two of Tyrone's All-Ireland winning team. However, I guarantee you, Danny, that they all know who Rebecca Loos is and who her sexual partners were. Are you happy for that situation to continue?

For the first time since 1995, when Jason Sherlock briefly lit up the sporting landscape, the GAA last year unearthed a very marketable star, even a sex symbol, in Setanta Ó hAilpín who could be used to bring the gospel of football and hurling to a whole new audience. Most of us are obliged to work hard for our place in the sun; others, like Setanta, have greatness thrust upon them. He has that rare, special talent that causes a quickening of the pulse. To add to the package he is also intelligent. You would never have a situation with him like the one that arose with David Beckham.

Journalist: Do you think you're a volatile player?
Becks: I suppose I am. I can play on the left or the right or in the middle.

I felt then, as I do now, that the GAA in Cork, and indeed nationally, should have done more to retain Setanta's services. Very rarely does a star like him come along in the GAA who can grab the imagination of Irish youth, male and female, and yet, after just one season, we let him travel halfway around the world away to Australia.

I know that the GAA is using some current and former inter-county footballers and hurlers as coaches and development officers, and I am happy to applaud them for that, but it is not enough. No matter how much we may despise it, the fact of the matter is that we live in an age of the cult of celebrity and Setanta is a publicist's dream. Here was a guy who, with proper marketing, could have been bigger than Harry Potter with the youth of Ireland. Yet the GAA seems to think that the old ways are sufficient and that what worked in the 1950s will still work today. At the risk of seeming conceited, I would say, Danny, that I am closer to the youth of Ireland than you. I know that there are no posters of GAA stars on their walls to go with their photos of Michael Owen, Jonny Wilkinson, Britney Spears and Beyoncé. Setanta would have opened new doors for the GAA with the young audience, but we did not exploit his potential as a marketing vehicle for our games. Who knows when a star like him will next appear on the scene? If previous experience is anything to go by, then the answer is not for a long time.

Hurling is such a skillful game, we should be doing everything in our power to showcase it. I played a bit of hurling myself. I gave it up, though, when one of my teachers was watching me playing a game with little success and he said to me, 'Cut five inches off your hurley.'

'Do you think my hurley is too big for me?' I asked.

Turning away he said, 'No, but it will fit into the bin much more easily.'

Setanta was someone who could have electrified the popularity of the sport. At the risk of offending your delicate sensibilities by using a soccer metaphor, I can only describe the GAA's inaction on Setanta as an own goal. As someone who spends my working day trying to encourage often apathetic teenagers to play Gaelic games, I find it inexcusable.

On a related matter, the GAA needs to show greater respect for inter-county players. Sure their lot has improved greatly in recent years, thanks mainly to the work of the GPA, however the Setanta Ó hAilpín case highlighted, yet again, the frustration felt by many players. Such are the demands being placed on them that they are out of pocket as a result of their efforts in the county jersey. When one of the country's star hurlers like Setanta opts to join a struggling Aussie Rules club in order to pursue his dream of becoming a professional sportsman, then the GAA has a problem.

Virtually since the foundation of the GAA, its success has been based on the work of its volunteers at grass-roots level in clubs and schools. Sadly, in modern Ireland, the volunteer 'species' is in free-fall. Nowadays the vast majority of primary school teachers are female and most of these have no interest in promoting Gaelic games. It is not quite as bad at secondary school level, but we are still heading in the wrong direction, as fewer and fewer teachers are prepared to train teams after school in the evening.

The problem is compounded in GAA clubs up and down the country. Rather than give something back to the game when they retire, the majority of players take to the golf course. They are lost to the GAA for the rest of their lives.

Clubs must share the blame, particularly the dominant clubs in the larger towns and cities. They are only interested in winning trophies and, as a result, pick the cream of the players. The majority of youngsters who are primarily interested in playing the game for enjoyment purposes are discarded and so are lost to the GAA.

Of course, the GAA itself at national level must take a lot of the blame too. For years its priorities have been arseways – spending vast amounts of money on building stadia and paying only lip service to coaching and games development. Unless the budgets spent by the GAA on these areas are vastly increased, the flight of our youth to other sports will continue. Yet, while we have reached crisis point, the situation is not beyond redemption. But the GAA must act immediately. Otherwise it will be a case of closing the stable door after the horse has bolted. That was my only concern in speaking about the Setanta affair. Those of us working on the ground to promote the games need a shot in the arm. We do not need the GAA to shoot itself in the foot.

Danny, as you proudly boast, the GAA '... will continue to do things their way and will not be dictated to by anyone'. My concern is that you mistake being 'dictated to' with listening to constructive criticism. Your tone of 'continuing to do things your way' smacks of complacency. You should know that if you rest on your laurels, they become funeral wreaths. Are you so certain that you and the boys in HQ have such a monopoly on wisdom that you can afford to shut two deaf ears to any alternative vision or lateral thinking? Or has the Pope invested not me but you and the GAA's ruling elite with infallibility?

The problem, Danny my friend, is that the GAA continues to be held back by administrators clinging to the rowing boats of the old ways and the mantra of amateurism. If it was good enough in their day ... it is certainly not good enough now.

Anyway, compliments of the season to you. May your days be merry and bright and may all your Christmases be white. Maybe then in the New Year you and your buddies in Croke Park will be more receptive to those of us who are trying to lead the GAA from darkness to light.

Your good friend and fellow Kerryman,

Pat

11

A Life Less Ordinary

There are two kinds of people: those who are from Kerry and those who want to be from Kerry. Football is to Kerry what films are to Hollywood: a county-wide obsession that sets a pecking order, discussed endlessly and by everyone, complete with its own arcane laws and rituals. Pubs are the churches of this strange sporting religion. Football-talk is no idle form of idle gossip here, but a crucial element in the county's psyche, to which business, love, the land and the weather regularly take second place.

We are very ecumenical, though, when it comes to sport. In August 2003, we saw a great day for Kerry sport when Gillian O'Sullivan won a silver medal in the European championships. Then that same afternoon we saw Kerry implode against Tyrone in the All-Ireland semifinal. It was like winning the Lotto and then immediately finding out that you had only 24 hours to live! Effectively it was the end of the road for Páidí Ó Sé's reign as Kerry manager.

Guardian of the Peace

Páidí was a year behind me in the Sem in Killarney. His passion for football was evident at an early stage, after Kerry beat Meath in the 1970 All-Ireland final. Páidí was a boarder, so it was not possible for him to legitimately attend the homecoming celebrations. He arranged to borrow a bike from one of the day students, robbed a brush and dressed it up as a decoy in his bed, and set out for Rathmore. When he returned, the College dean,

Dermot Clifford, now Archbishop of Cashel, was waiting for him at the entrance. 'Ó Sé,' he said, 'there are more brains in that brush above than in your head.'

Páidí is a good story-teller and is well able to tell stories against himself. Many go back to his time as a garda. One night in 1979, after a League match against Cork, Páidí went on the tear. The next morning when he went in to report for duty in Limerick, he was feeling a bit off colour. He decided that the best way to conceal his discomfort was to take out the squad car and pretend to go on patrol, but instead he pulled into a quiet field for a nap. A few hours later Páidí was awoken by a great commotion to find that there were squad cars all over the field. He stumbled out of the car and came face to face with the Assistant Commissioner who asked, 'Páidí, did you nod off for a little while?'

'I'm sorry. I'd an auld game yesterday and I just pulled in for a few minutes. What are all of ye doing here?'

'We're checking out the venue for the Pope's visit to Limerick next September. The Holy Father'll be saying a Mass out here. We're sussin' out the place for the security plan. Sorry to have disturbed you.'

After a shift ended, it was customary for a garda to go out for a drink. Sometimes, though, this posed problems when the session carried on after closing hours. Early in his career, Páidí was dispatched one night to inspect a pub that was reportedly selling alcohol after hours. When he arrived at the premises, he was told to check it out before entering. 'I'm here now, over,' he radioed back to the station.

'Is there any activity there?' questioned the officer.

'Yes,' Páidí replied. 'I can hear people shouting, I can hear laughter and I can hear glasses clinking.'

'And can you hear a cash register going?' asked the officer.

'No,' Páidí replied.

'Ah, you better leave it off Garda Ó Sé, it could be our own crowd.'

Fear Crua

I think some players today are too pampered and have lost the steel you need to make it to the very top. Some players are so injury prone, they would go straight on the sick list if they met one of the lads in the Artane Boys band. Páidí, though, was as tough as teak.

When Dublin played Kerry in 1978 in New York as a fundraiser for Sr Consilio, the match was the most physically violent in living memory. A lot of old scores had to be settled and markers were put down for the Championship later that year. Legen has it that Pat O'Neill broke Jimmy Deenihan's nose. Afterwards O'Neill was very contrite and later that night he sent an apology to Deenihan in the Kerry hotel. He told him he was very sorry and had never intended to hurt him, he had thought he was striking Páidí Ó Sé!

In 1985 everyone on the Kerry team had their heart set on winning the All-Ireland again. None more so than Páidí, as he was captain. As Páidí was trying to gee up the troops before the game, he said, 'We really need to win this one.'

Mick O'Dwyer asked, 'For who?'

'For me.'

'Not for Kerry?'

'Well, for Kerry as well.'

In an effort to add impact to his words, Páidí smashed the ball as hard as he could on the ground. It bounced so high that it shattered the lights overhead. Glass flew all over the dressing-room. Yet so absorbed were the team in the team talk that not a single player noticed the incident.

Páidí always enjoyed the social side of the game too. In the 1970s and 1980s winning All-Irelands became such a routine that, as we ran on to Croke Park after Mick O'Dwyer had been trying to psyche us up to play the game of our lives before an All-Ireland final, John Egan ran up and pulled Páidí Ó Sé by the togs and asked him, 'Where are ye going after the game, Páidí?'

You've Lost that Winning Feeling

Páidí, like myself, is a media animal. He wears his heart on his sleeve, but he is a lot cuter than most people give him credit for. People make him out to be blood, guts, shouting and roaring, and passion, and he is all that, but he is much more.

Having said that, I was watching him being interviewed on the sideline after Westmeath's victory over Dublin and he was very passionate, which is great, but he had a jugular vein that was on the point of bursting. If I had any doubts about whether I should have gone into management, they died in that moment.

When people talk about the great managers of today, they speak about John O'Mahony and Seán Boylan, but Páidí's record compares favourably with anybody. He did bring a National League and under-21 All-Ireland to Kerry and two All-Irelands in 1997 and 2000. He kept Westmeath in Division One of the League and took them to their first ever Leinster title. I think people who doubted Páidí's credentials when he was appointed Kerry manager have been proved wrong. I am not alone in believing that Páidí has been completely underestimated as a manager. Everyone knows his passion, but what many people miss out on is his astute and cunning footballing brain. We saw it this year in the switches he made for Westmeath against Dublin. Also he brought an All-Ireland to Kerry in 1997 with what I have publicly stated was the poorest team to ever win an All-Ireland.

The wheels came off the wagon in the 2001 All-Ireland semifinal, when Meath beat Kerry by no less than 15 points. Kerry went through a 29-minute spell in the first half without scoring and then could only muster a single point from substitute Declan Quill in the second half. After the match, Marty Morrissey asked a Kerry fan 'Where did it all go wrong in Croke Park today?'

The fan replied, 'The green bit in the middle.'

Inevitably when a Kerry team loses by 15 points in Croke Park, serious questions were asked, particularly when Páidí refused to start Maurice Fitzgerald. You can train for all conscious eventualities, but your greatest moments are when your instinct takes over and afterwards you cannot remotely explain why you did what you did. My moment like that as a player came in the goal I scored in the 1986 All-Ireland final against Tyrone, when I dived into the air to palm the ball into the net. To this day I still don't know why I did it that way. Maurice's career is peppered with far more moments of genius than I ever produced. His finest hour was the 1997 All-Ireland, when he regularly broke through with Mayo defenders falling around him like dying wasps and kicked incredible points from all angles. There was a time I would have joked that if my mother had been marking Pat Holmes that day she would have been man of the match. Not any more! Let us instead simply observe that Pat made Maurice's job a lot easier that day. Along with Mike Sheehy, Maurice was the most skilful player I ever played with in the Kerry jersey.

Maurice is very quiet. However, some of the people surrounding him liked publicity. He had two very high profile people backing him in the media: GOAL's John O'Shea and the editor of the *Sunday Independent*, Aengus Fanning. The people advising him had Maurice's best interests in mind, but not necessarily the best interests of Kerry football, although they purported to have the good of Kerry football at heart.

You can argue that Páidí was right or wrong but at the end of the day Páidí *was* proved right. There is a very thin line between success and failure, and on the basis of your decisions you have to be judged on whether you were right or wrong. Páidí was proved right in 2000. Maurice was most effective as an impact sub. It was a big gamble but it delivered an All-Ireland.

I was looking forward to reading Páidí's autobiography, because I thought it would be the perfect opportunity for him to finally tell us what his problem with Maurice Fitzgerald was, but on the single issue that most exercised Kerry people he said absolutely nothing. Ronan Keating was wrong. You do not say it best when you say nothing at all.

No football manager is an island. He needs a good team behind him, on and off the field. It would also have been nice to read the real story of Páidí's relationship with John O'Keeffe. Johno is a lovely guy and a real gentleman. Initially it seemed Páidí wouldn't be given the Kerry job because people thought he was a loose cannon, but these people underestimated him. When Páidí first started, he was given Seamus McGearailt to 'mind' him. There is no doubt that Seamus kept Páidí under control and made a massive contribution to Kerry's success in 1997. What people don't realise though is that, if Páidí was unsure about anything, he was always willing to get advice. However, he would do this indirectly and not ask anyone close to the Kerry camp. When Seamus moved on, Johno was parachuted in, as certain people thought Páidí was incapable of training the team on his own. The nature of this imposition put a strain on their relationship straight away. A comparable relationship would have been that of Eddie O'Sullivan and Declan Kidney. At the best of times Johno and Páidí would not have been bosom pals.

The two big controversies of Páidí's reign – the Maurice and Johno situations and the 'animals' controversy (when he called Kerry fans f***ing animals) – were played out in the full glare of the media. He was unlucky insofar as the animals controversy blew up at a very quiet time of the year when there was nothing else for GAA journalists to write about, and, as we all know, paper never refuses ink.

A lot of Páidí's most vocal critics were people with agendas. His interview in South Africa was ill-advised. It was not good for Kerry football to have its dirty linen washed in public, nor to have colleagues and former colleagues on opposite sides. There were no winners in that situation and it left a bitter legacy and a sour taste.

Páidí, Ambrose O'Donovan and Ger Lynch were my best friends on the Kerry team. Páidí was very kind to me in his book. I used to joke with him that if he was nasty to me in the book I would pay him back big time in the *Sunday World*! I think it worked!

Not Captain Fantastic

Páidí took the Meath defeat in 2001 very badly. A few days after the match, he went into the church in Ventry in Co. Kerry and said a prayer to St Jude. He prayed that Kerry would again become the dominant team in Gaelic football as they had been in the late 1970s. He got an awful shock when a great voice boomed down from heaven: 'I know I'm the patron saint of hopeless causes, but not even I can swing that for you Páidí.'

A friend of mine put the scale of the disappointment in Kerry well: 'It was like thinking you have gone to bed with Liz Hurley only to wake up to the terrible realisation that you have slept with Red Hurley.'

I was reminded of that match early in January of this year. It was obviously a slow week in Kerry as Joe O'Mahony from Radio Kerry asked me to go on the radio to talk about the decision to appoint Dara Ó Cinnéide as Kerry captain. I knew immediately that I was only being asked on to stir up trouble. Our club, Templenoe, had put in a motion that, in the future, all Kerry captains be selected by management. My feeling was that Dara would not always make it on to the first 15. There was going to be trouble and we would be back to square one. Sure enough in Kerry's opening game in the Championship, Dara was on the bench. Dara had a real rollercoaster of a year. He was on and off the team, and there was uncertainty about whether he would be seleced for the All-Ireland. In the end, he was, and he had an excellent game. It is just another reminder that perserverance pays off.

We were trying to avoid that situation where the county champions pick the captain. That is all very well in theory, but a major problem arises when the county champions do not have a player on the county team. We wanted to ensure that the wrong guys were not selected as captain. In 2003, the county champions, Kerins O'Rahilly, had no one from their own club so they appointed a captain from the beaten finalists, Kilcummin. They selected Mike McCarthy. Mike is a lovely guy but very introverted, which is the last type of personality you want as captain. You want an Anthony Daly type who is going to rally the troops, or someone like Kieran McGeeney or Peter Canavan who are both natural leaders, outstanding footballers and very intelligent guys who can read the game, eliminating the necessity for managers running onto the field to get messages to their players.

In 2001, Dr Crokes were county champions. They did not initially have a player on the county team and Seamus Moynihan, as the most experienced player on the team, was appointed captain. That year Kerry got to the All-Ireland semifinal against Meath – a game no one in Kerry will ever forget because of the trouncing we got.

A representative from Dr Crokes, Eoin Brosnan, eventually got on the team. As was their right, Dr Crokes insisted that Brosnan be appointed captain. He was to play his first game in Croke Park in an important match and he did not need that pressure. We all know that with so little between teams now, it is vital to have a good leader on the team, particularly in the new ground in Croke Park where managers complain that it is impossible to give messages from the sideline.

So when Radio Kerry asked me on, I declined to offer any opinion at all – which was a first!

Magic Moments

Until 2004, Kerry had not had much to be proud of, but we liked to think that Páidí was the greatest magician of all time. He made Kerry disappear for the entire second half of the 2002 All-Ireland final against Armagh.

An old joke was revisited: 'Why aren't the Kerry team allowed to own a dog? Because they can't hold on to a lead.'

The 2002 All-Ireland final, a classic case of nouveau riche versus old money, is a match I will never be allowed to forget. Don't think I haven't tried. At half-time I was 'sceptical' about Armagh's chances of beating Kerry. I caused consternation among Armagh fans when I said, 'My mother has arthritis, but even she has more pace than the Armagh full-back line.' In the second half I was left looking a right idiot and, understandably, one banner featured prominently in the subsequent media coverage. Against a backdrop of the Armagh colours it simply said, 'Are you watching, Pat Spillane?'

Three days later, when Armagh played Louth in the GOAL challenge, a large man dressed up in drag, in the Kerry colours, and wearing a placard stating that he was 'Pat Spillane's Ma', challenged each of the full-back line to an individual race. 'She' won each time.

I hoped my embarrassment would take some of the pressure off Páidí and the boys, but not so. A few weeks later, a man was driving home from a night in the pub. He was pulled in by a guard.

The guard said, 'I'm going to have to get you to blow into the bag.'

The driver pulled out a card from his pocket which read: 'Asthmatic. Don't take breath samples.'

The guard said, 'I'm going to have to take a sample of your blood.'

He took out another card from his pocket: 'Haemophiliac. Don't take blood samples.'

The guard said, 'I'm going to have to take a urine sample.'

The motorist took out another card from his pocket. This one read: 'Member of Kerry supporters club. Don't take the piss.'

One of the virtues of Kerry people is that we can laugh at ourselves. Kerry people are quite thick-skinned, not sensitive and enjoy a good joke. I have no problem at all when people make jokes at my expense. My wife often remarks that it is a great job that I can laugh at myself because I have so many reasons to!

Peter the Great

Most people thought that Kerry had underachieved in the previous two years, but that 2003 was going to be the year that Kerry made up for lost time and reclaimed the Sam Maguire trophy. Fate was destined to booby-trap Kerry once again that summer, however.

Before the All-Ireland semifinal between Kerry and Tyrone, Seamus Moynihan faced an apparently impossible task of marking the mighty Peter Canavan. Before the game, Moynihan had an unusual tactical talk with Páidí Ó Sé. Páidí asked, 'Right, Seamus, how are we going to deal with this guy, Peter Canavan?'

'Okay, Páidí, I'm gonna angle my run so I push him towards the touch-line and use it as an extra man, just forcing him out for a lineball.'

'Okay. But what happens if he cuts inside you?'

'Well, I'll angle it so that he's running back towards our cover defence, and the other backs will be there to help smother him and dispossess him.'

'Great. But what happens if he runs straight at you?'

'Okay, if he runs straight at me, I'll get some crap off the ground and throw it in his face, blinding him.'

'What? But there won't be any crap on the ground.'

'If he's running straight at me, Páidí, yes there will!'

A week after the match, which saw another spectacular Kerry defeat, a Tyrone and Kerry fella were being executed together. The executioner says to them both, 'I'll grant you one last wish before I hang you.'

The Tyrone fella says, 'I'm from Tyrone. We beat Kerry in the All-Ireland semifinal a few days ago, and I'd like to go to my death after watching those magic moments once again.'

The guard said, 'No problem. We'll wheel out a big screen and you can watch the game again.'

Then he turned to the Kerry man and asked him what his last wish was. The Kerry man replied, 'Hang me first.'

While Kerry people sat at home and watched Tyrone win the All-Ireland, my two neighbours had a revealing conversation:

'I saw the Kerry team on television last night with the Sam Maguire trophy.'

'What programme was it?'

'*Crimeline.*'

Love Me Tender

Once upon a time I could give speeches about the greatness of Kerry football, but after Meath in 2001, Armagh in 2002 and Tyrone in 2003, I have been forced to be humble. It is not a role that I'm comfortable with!

Over those three years, it was hard to boast about our football team in Kerry. One of the few things we have left to boast about is our lovemaking. A Kerry man, a Cork man and a Dub were having a discussion on a plane.

The Dub said, 'Last night I made love to my wife 20 times. This morning she told me I was the greatest lover of all time. She gave me Bewley's coffee and cooked me the biggest Irish breakfast that you have ever seen.'

The Cork guy said, 'Last night I made love to my wife 25 times. This morning she said I was the greatest lover of all time.

She gave me Barry's tea and cooked me the biggest mixed grill of all time.'

The Cork and Dublin fellas turned to their companion from Kerry who was being remarkably reticent. They asked him how many times he had made love to his wife the previous night. When he replied that it was only once they had a great laugh at him. 'What did she say to you this morning?' asked the Dub.

The Kerry man replied, 'Why are you stopping now?'

Get Smart

Apparently shortly before he died, someone suggested to John B. Keane that he should write a play on Páidí Ó Sé's reign as Kerry manager. 'I don't write tragedies,' he replied.

Where did it all go wrong for Kerry in Páidí's last three years? There are a number of different theories on success. George Best's recipe for success with women was: 'Don't drink, don't smoke, don't be too particular.' I believe, though, that there are only two things you need to succeed as a football manager and in life.

First, you need common sense. A few years ago the Americans experienced a setback to their space programme. They discovered that they did not have a biro that worked on moon landings. Over the next few years they made correcting this problem a priority. They spent 12 billion dollars on inventing a pen that would work in any environment on earth, under water and in space. What did the Russians do? They used a pencil.

In a lot of counties, common sense went out the window in Gaelic football with managers having their teams doing adventure courses and doing weight training like Olympic weight-lifters. There is no logic in having so many training sessions without the ball. Football is a game with a ball and to become good at it, players must learn how to use the ball.

The second thing you need for success is an ability to read and adapt to a situation. The successful sportsperson and business person can size up a situation and react as the circumstances demand. A parable illustrates this. A Kerry man who was going on a plane to San Francisco and found himself sitting beside a beautiful blonde. He asked her where she was going. 'I'm going to the World Nymphomaniac Conference,' she replied.

The man's curiosity was aroused and he asked, 'Business or pleasure?'

'Business.'

'What business exactly?'

'I'm in the business of trying to disprove certain myths that surround sexuality.'

'What would these myths be?'

'The first myth is that the African-American is the most well-endowed person in the world. That's not true. It's the native American. The second myth is that the French are the world's greatest lovers. Actually, it's the Irish.'

'Really?'

'Yes, but I shouldn't be talking to you about this. I'm sure you find it embarrassing.'

'Oh no, not at all. I'm fascinated by the subject. What's your name by the way?'

'Ulkria Keane. What's yours?'

'Tonto Murphy.'

When the going got tough for Kerry in Croke Park in successive years against Meath, Armagh and Tyrone, Páidí was unable to come up with a plan B to reverse the situation.

The players must also take their share of their blame, however. The hallmark of a great player is one who knows when his usual ploy isn't working and can adjust his game according to the circumstances. The players on the great Kerry team could do that because they were very intelligent and could read games well, and adapt and change tactics when needed. The great captain is one who can motivate his troops and can sort things out with a calm head when they are not going according to plan on the pitch. In recent years there has been a clamour for 'runners' on the field in Croke Park. Runners can give the manager's instructions because they find it impossible to communicate with their players from the sideline due to the noise. That is why they need a captain who can read a situation on pitch. The classic example of this was Tony Hanahoe. Tony was the thinking man's footballer.

The wounds from those three losses cut deeply, not because we lost, but because we lost so tamely on each occasion. That is not the Kerry way. To lose abysmally once was bad; for it to happen twice was shocking, but for it to happen to Kerry three years in a row in Croke Park, the ground we think of as our second home, was the end of the world. In some counties, success is accidental. In Kerry it is compulsory. After failing so spectacularly three years in a row, Páidí's days were numbered. The only problem was that Páidí himself didn't see it that way.

Quote, Unquote

The year 2003 was Páidí's year of the U-turn. In January he had an interview with the *Sunday Independent* and famously said, 'Being the Kerry manager is probably the hardest job in the world because Kerry people, I'd say, are the roughest type of f*****g animals you could deal with. And you can print that.' A short time later he was forced to meekly apologise: 'I regret very much if I have offended all or some of my Kerry supporters who have been very loyal to me.'

Then, after his reluctant departure as Kerry manager in October, he said, 'I wouldn't rule anything in or out, but I couldn't see myself at the present time having the bottle to go in and train another team against the green and gold jersey.'

A week later, after taking over as Westmeath manager, he said, 'I now want to transfer all my professional allegiance to Westmeath and will endeavour to coach and improve the team and achieve success in the future.'

'Is the glass half empty or half full?' I asked Páidí.

'It depends on whether you are drinking or pouring,' he replied.

After Westmeaths' inauspicious League campaign, I was sceptical of Westmeath's chances. On 18 April, 2004, in my column in the *Sunday World*, I divided counties into various categories. One of my five no-hopers was Westmeath. I wrote:

> One would not normally expect a team who managed to avoid relegation from Division One to be parked here. But Westmeath's Houdini-like escape from relegation had precious little to do with their own ability and more to do with other counties shooting themselves in the foot, notably Longford, who would have stayed up and put Westmeath down had they managed to beat Fermanagh at home. This is looking like a temporary little management arrangement for Páidí.

I had no doubts before the Championship that Westmeath were going nowhere. I'm always like that. I may often be wrong, but I never have any doubts!

Getting predictions wrong does not faze me unduly. I always get my predictions wrong and a few times a week I will meet people who will say something like: 'Spillane you're only a chancer. You know nothing about football. You were wrong again last Sunday.' On such occasions I always quote the line of the Declan Nerney song: 'If I knew then what I know now, I'd be a wiser man.'

The great thing is that RTÉ pay me to come and tell the nation what I think will happen on *The Sunday Game*. Then, when I make a dog's dinner of it and get it badly wrong, the *Sunday World* pay me the following Sunday to explain why I got it so wrong!

To add insult to injury, Westmeath beat Dublin in the Leinster quarter-final. I had confidently slotted the Dubs in as number two, behind Laois, on my list of 'Glory Hunters'.

Rogue's Gallery

Páidí, Micko and I are all cut from the same cloth. We're all rogues! It is possible we were not blessed with the greatest talent as players, but we have football coursing through our veins, are passionate about the game, and are well able to grasp any opportunities that present themselves on or off the field.

Both Páidí and Micko are still hurting from the circumstances surrounding their departure from the Kerry job. The pair are masters of the spin. No PR guru in the country could hold the candle to them in this field. Hyping up the opposition and playing down their own team's chances is their specialist subject. The only difference is that Micko has been codding the nation 30 years longer than Páidí. However, the public are still swallowing it. Both are driven men who believe their team is only as good as their last performance.

Talking about Bertie Ahern during the summer of 2004, Charlie McCreevy said he knew about 25 per cent of Bertie, which, he suggested, was 24 per cent more than anybody else. I feel the same about Páidí.

I rang Páidí after the Leinster final to congratulate him on Westmeath's victory. In fairness he simply said, 'We got the rub of the relic all the year long.' Winning teams get the rub of the relic.

For once O'Dwyer didn't get it right in the Leinster final replay in 2004. Laois looked like a team that was mentally and physically jaded. That would have been acceptable had they won a couple of All-Irelands, but all this team has won is one Leinster title. The fact that Mick Lawlor and Colm Byrne walked away from the panel before coming back again was not a good sign, and their flat performance against Tyrone confirmed that things were not as they should be.

Páidí has no need to employ psychologists. When he speaks to his players, he does so authoritatively, having achieved so much as a player and manager at the highest level. Any self-respecting player will heed what he has to say because he's been there and done that. I despair when I hear managers employing so-called sports psychologists because I believe it is a sign of weakness as in my experience they are generally just guys who have swallowed American books and American jargon about motivation. That is not what you need to win things. What you need to do as a manager is to get your team to play with commitment and belief. Páidí brought Westmeath to their first Leinster title because he was able to do that.

I found it interesting that in the same weekend Páidí was steering Westmeath to glory, Dinny Cahill was using reverse psychology with the Antrim hurlers. Before he criticised Brian Corcoran and Niall McCarthy, Dinny should have remembered that he who throws mud loses ground. All he succeeded in doing was in revving up Cork. It is easy for someone like Dinny to come out with bold talk before a match, but unless you are able to back it up it is just bravado.

In 1995 at half-time during the All-Ireland final, Ger Loughnane said, 'We're going to do it.' As I watched him I was convinced. Páidí needs neither gimmicks nor experts to back him up when he speaks to the Westmeath players because he has conviction and gravitas, and he talks with the voice of authoritative experience. If someone claiming to be a sports psychologist started telling me what I should be thinking and doing when I was playing, I would have asked him, 'Excuse me, how many All-Irelands have you won, then?'

As a sporting ecumenist, the same weekend as Westmeath won their Leinster title, I was also watching the Nissan Irish Open at Baltray on television. Brett Rumford got over €300,000 for winning. Every time those wealthy, pampered golfers wanted to go even the shortest distance there were courtesy cars to take them. All the Westmeath players got was a medal and a cup. In financial terms, the Westmeath supporters got nothing. Yet when

Rumford made his final putt and was presented with his trophy there was merely polite applause whereas when the final whistle blew after the Leinster final replay there was an explosion of emotions: elation, pride, relief and communal joy. There have been few matches that have unleashed a greater flood of excitement and pleasure than the Westmeath victory. The eruption of euphoria was a sight to put a tingle in the blood. This is why Gaelic games are so magical.

Flying High

Given the desire for success in Westmeath I wasn't surprised when their County Board pulled out all the stops, and according to popular belief, their cheque book to lure Páidí to the county. Obviously under GAA rules they can only give money for expenses and we all know how strictly they adhere to that rule.

There are lots of rumours about all the money Páidí is getting from Westmeath for doing the job. Earlier this year I was contacted by a journalist from a major newspaper. 'We're going to run a story exposing the fact that Páidí is making so much money from Westmeath,' he said.

'Have ye proof?' I asked.

'No. But everybody says he is.'

'Is there a paper-trail there?'

'No.'

It was typical: *'Duirt bean liom go nduirt bean léi.'*

The bottom line is that we can speculate on a figure that Páidí is getting, but if you just tot up mileage expenses from Ventry to Mullingar a few times a week, you would get a massive sum. As nobody could prove anything, the story was not published.

My view is that whatever Páidí is getting, he's worth every penny because he raised the profile of the game within the county, really putting Westmeath on the football map by taking them to their first-ever Leinster title in his first season. He created a buzz within the county and a feeling of togetherness and identity, and now more and more youngsters are wearing the Westmeath jersey.

I have no problem with high-profile managers because they are good for boosting the profile of the game. If they can bring in extra crowds they will generate a lot more money than they actually take out.

I heard another story that Páidí is supposed to be getting a helicopter to fly him from Kerry to Westmeath for training sessions. During our days on the Kerry team, Páidí had an amazing fear of flying. Paudie Lynch shared that fear and when we were travelling on trips abroad the two of them coped by getting totally inebriated before the trip.

I remember one day when we got to Dublin airport I said, 'Look here Páidí, if it's your day to go, it's your day to go.'

Páidí turned around to me and said, 'But if it's the f*****g pilot's day to go, he's going to bring me down with him!'

When Pat Nearly Met Charlie

I have to confess that I am completely awestruck by Páidí Ó Sé's business acumen. This is most evident in the incredible hype and publicity he generates for his football tournament. He can get a lengthy prime time interview on the Marian Finucane show to plug it. He can get the Taoiseach to launch it. He can get the Artane Boys band to provide the music in the Burlington Hotel. He can get half the cabinet and another 30 TDs and 20 of the top business people in Dublin to the launch of what is essentially a Micky Mouse tournament. Páidí can sell it as the greatest thing since the Superbowl and get massive sponsorship for it.

Páidí is a great man for capitalising on his contacts. Down the years he has made the most of his friendship with Charlie Haughey. The much-missed *Scrap Saturday* programme regularly lampooned Charlie for his willingness to claim ancestry from every county in the land. Charlie has completely gone to town, though on his special relationship with Kerry, and part of the image he projects is that he is a great connoisseur of Kerry football. Over the years, Charlie and Páidí used each other, but Páidí reaped the greatest dividend from their association. He was best able to maximise the relationship to his own advantage.

The two men have a lot in common as neither is short on self-confidence. Charlie presented himself as a great statesman on the world stage. And Páidí does not believe that you should hide your light under a bushel either. A visitor to his pub observed that only a North Korean dictator has as many photos of themselves as Páidí does. When he takes tourists from America to Páidí's, the local taxi driver always tells them that the church beside the pub is built as a shrine to Páidí. When they see all the photos in the pub, they believe him.

Páidí captained Kerry to the All-Ireland in 1985. The following morning, Páidí brought my brother, Tom, and a few of the other lads out to meet Charlie in Kinsealy. Sadly though I missed out on my own meeting with Charlie Haughey. I came very close. I was in the Skellig Hotel in Dingle the morning after the Dingle Regatta, and Charlie and his entourage were coifing champagne. They were loud and boisterous and I heard one of them say, 'There's Pat Spillane over there.'

Charlie swanned over to the table beside me and tapped a man on the shoulder and said, 'Pat Spillane, I presume?'

The astonished guy replied, 'I wish.'

Charlie turned on his heels and walked back to his party as if nothing had happened. So much for his great knowledge of Kerry football.

12

The Lyons Den

In the Emmy award-winning series *The Office*, David Brent called a staff meeting to announce job cuts. 'There's good news and bad news. The bad news is that some of you will lose your jobs. I know: gutting. On a more positive note, the good note, the good news is: I've been promoted! So every cloud has a silver lining.' In many ways that story is a symptom of what is wrong with a lot of Gaelic football managers today. The cult of the manager has become all powerful. In many cases when they win, they take the credit, but when they lose it is their players who get the blame. Now if you get a couple of bad results, you are gone.

In the last two years, the manager who has been most in the firing line has been the Dublin manager, Tommy Lyons. The same critics who were throwing bouquets at Tommy in 2002 were swinging cleavers the following year. Some of the criticism was of such persistence and hostility it would have made Nixon wince. After Dublin lost to Laois and Armagh in 2003, Tommy's fall from grace was reflected in the comment of one former Dublin player: 'The only way Tommy Lyons can get up again is with Viagra.'

Dub-le Trouble

Tommy is a good friend of mine. He came to the Dublin job with ambition you could sharpen knives on. To be a good manager you need to be such an optimist that you believe that when your shoes wear out, you will be back on your feet. Tommy seemed like a man who could inspire a donkey to win the derby.

In his first year, his optimism was justified when Dublin won the Leinster title. Dublin were a 'nearly team' that year and were unlucky to lose against Armagh. There is a very thin line between laughter and loss. Who will ever forget Ray Cosgrove's free coming off the post at the end? The problem is, as we say in Kerry, nearly never bulled a cow. Emperor Napoleon used to ask his aspiring generals whether they were lucky. Sporting champions need their fair share of luck too. The weather and the toss of a coin can make a huge difference, dictating surfaces, ends and directions. The wind is arbitrary, the sun has no favourites, the rain, like the tide, waits for no one. Even the best-prepared manager can't prevent his star player from pulling his hamstring or breaking his leg or missing an easy free. In such situations hopes of All-Ireland glory can vanish in an instant.

Dublin fans look back at 2002 as a golden era. It must also have been the year they all bought rose-tinted spectacles because Dublin were heavily reliant on the goals of Ray Cosgrove. Their problem is that they have too many forwards who wouldn't get a kick in a stampede.

After the defeat to Armagh in the Qualifiers in 2003, Tommy came out in front of the media and had a go at his own player, Stephen Cluxton, who had been sent off, for, in effect, costing the Dubs the game.

Tommy's critics say that he hung Cluxton out to dry and humiliated him, and that he broke the golden rule that you must never give out about a player outside the dressing-room. Tommy will maintain otherwise. He would say that if Cluxton deserved to be sent off then he should have been, and he hadn't seen the video evidence when he gave his now infamous interview to Jim Carney. I thought it was a good interview and I genuinely don't think Tommy hung Cluxton out to dry. When you interview a losing manager immediately after such a big game, when the stakes are so high, he isn't thinking rationally. Instead he's wounded and emotional, and you can't expect a detached, clinical analysis with total objectivity.

One thing always puzzled me about that affair, however. Before the sending off, Dublin were in the ascendancy and they seemed likely to win, but after the sending off, the wheels came off the Dublin wagon. Afterwards Tommy was vilified. Cluxton got away scott-free in terms of public criticism even though his sending off probably cost Dublin an All-Ireland appearance. Yet Cluxton became the victim and Tommy Lyons the villain. Strangely when watching Tommy making those comments about Cluxton, I thought of Ger Loughnane.

The Man From Clare

Loughnane is a legend from his days as Clare manager and for the many antics and controversies he was involved in. What people don't always adequately appreciate, though, is just how sharp his brain is.

I always remember a conversation I had with a very senior producer in RTÉ about Loughnane. The producer told me that he had been down with RTÉ at the infamous meeting of the Munster Council on 7 August 1998, which was to adjudicate on the notorious Colin Lynch affair. Lynch himself was unable to attend because that evening his grandmother had suffered a serious health setback and was dying.

The meeting was held in the Limerick Inn and there was an incredible atmosphere. There were 120 Clare people there to show their support. There were camera crews and media. Loughnane was there to speak on Lynch's behalf, but the Munster Council knew from previous experience that if he was let in there would be a serious confrontation. They decided to give Lynch a three months suspension. There were still Clare people in the foyer. The rumour was that the Munster Council delegates went out through the window to escape them.

Loughnane was in the back-room waiting all night. At one stage he got a call. It was Colin Lynch's aunt who asked, 'Do you know that Marty Morrissey has just announced on the television that Colin's grandmother is dead?' Loughnane apologised profusely to her for the distress the inaccuracy had caused the family. He went out and saw that this senior producer in RTÉ who was telling me the story was there. Loughane asked him, 'Where is Marty Morrisey?' Lucky for Marty he had already gone – I'd say Loughnane would have killed him. Poor Marty was very upset. When he discovered his mistake he went to the hospital to apologise to the Lynch family in person.

The producer involved told me in vivid detail what it was like to be accosted by Loughnane in this way. Loughnane was livid and as the producer describes it, 'the white in his eyes were showing'. It was the typical Loughnane mad mode. For a full 20 minutes he berated the RTÉ man about the station's treatment of Lynch. Being cornered by Loughnane in that way for 20 minutes when he was so hyped up is not an experience anybody would ever want to go through. Yet the producer told me that when he reflected about it afterwards, he realised what was amazing about the tirade was that Loughnane never once used bad language nor did he repeat himself once. When you think of the pressure he was under and the emotion of the time, it just shows how controlled a man Loughnane is. Tommy Lyons could have done with that control after the Armagh game.

Every time I meet Loughnane, I wind him up by saying the only reason Clare won anything in the 1990s was because of his assistant Mike MacNamara. It doesn't go down well.

I enjoy having a drink with Loughnane. My favourite story about him is that after Clare won the All-Ireland in 1995, he went to the travel agent and said, 'We've won the All-Ireland, after our first victory in the All-Ireland final for 81 years. We've plenty of money raised, we can go anywhere in the world. I've only one stipulation. We need to go somewhere where nobody knows anything about hurling.'

The travel agent replied: 'Sir, you have two choices, Thailand or Tipperary.'

Warning Signs

In the court of popular opinion, the League has become a more accurate barometer of a team's likely performance in the Championship than in my playing days. Early this year Dublin beat Tyrone, and in the process gave us all a clue about how to beat Tyrone. You fight fire with fire and you hit them hard. Unfortunately Dublin decided that that was the key game and decided not really to bother much in the League after that.

In contrast the opening match in the League brought a doomsday scenario for Kerry – go to Longford with new management in the opening game of the League and, horror of horrors, lose in injury time. I was talking with the County Chairman the next evening, and he told me that he had been crossing the street in Tralee when a man pulled up alongside him in his car and demanded Jack O'Connor's immediate resignation. A few months later, O'Connor steered Kerry to the League title.

In the second round of the League, Dublin only scored three points against Mayo. It is interesting to note that Tipperary's Declan Browne scored 1 goal and 19 points after the first two matches in the National League. That is more than the combined score of either Dublin, Clare, London, Cork, Wexford, Armagh, Laois or Fermanagh.

The next night, the Dub fans were on air in their droves. *Sportscall* is an amazing programme, particularly when Dublin GAA supporters have a rant about their team and/or management, which is fairly often. The previous week Tommy Lyons was a saint. This week he was vilified from all angles. One fan suggested that he be replaced by John O'Leary. What?! Is that guy for real? This is the same John O'Leary who turned Wicklow into the worst county team in the country in 2002 and 2003.

To be Dublin manager today is probably an impossible position. Tommy was, however, the architect of some of his own problems by taking too much of the credit for Dublin's performances in 2002 when they won the Leinster title. One defeat in the League and people were calling for his head. Cockiness is no crime, especially in a world where undue reticence is a recipe for being left behind, but Gaelic games is one of the areas where the penalties for overdosing on self-approval are especially severe. What amazed me is that people forgot 2002 so quickly and also that Lyons had steered the Dubs to the All-Ireland under-21 title in 2003. Memories are very short. Tommy's record can stand with anyone's. Dublin fans should recall that he also led Kilmacud Crokes to an All-Ireland. He also took Offaly to a League and Leinster title playing a very attractive brand of football. At the time the secret of Offaly's success was supposed to be the Neutron diet, a panacea to end all bulging waistlines. Whatever happened to the Neutron diet?

One Tommy Lyons fan sought revenge on *Sportscall* recently, saying, most unfairly, that the radio show, 'is to nutcases as statues are to birdsh*t: a convenient platform upon which to deposit badly digested ideas.' Another description of it is that it is 'like skiing – it goes downhill fast'.

It's Good to Talk

In 2002, I presented *Sportscall* for much of the summer. It's an amazing thing in Ireland that everyone has an opinion on sport, politics and religion. Getting people on the air to talk about sport is easy, and *Sportscall* works so well because it is driven by the listeners.

When I was invited to present the *Sportscall* programme on RTÉ I went up early in the morning. I was certain I was going to be well trained before the programme started on studio control, on how to use all the gadgetry and technology, on voice projection and all that kind of thing.

My preparation for prime time radio went as follows:

- With 10 minutes to go to air I am sitting on a studio chair not knowing what is going on.
- With eight minutes to air a woman walks into the studio. She looks at the computer. It is not on. She hits it and eventually something comes up on the screen.
- Five minutes to air a sound man comes in and says, 'Press that button and shout into it.' I press the button and say a few sentences. I now know that this is what is known in the business as a sound-check.
- Three minutes to go. The producer comes in and tells me that there are no phone calls in yet, but just to keep talking and eventually something will come up on the screen.

That was my introduction to *Sportscall*, a prime time programme on national radio. I sat in for Des Cahill for the summer just after the Roy Keane controversy during the World Cup in 2002. It was like going to the well when all the water has been drained because every Tom, Dick and Harriet had expressed their opinion to Joe Duffy, Marian Finucane, Pat Kenny and Gerry Ryan. Anyone who wanted to give their viewpoint had already done so.

The Bachelors from Westmeath

With my finger on the pulse as ever, I had confidently predicted that Dublin would win the Leinster final in 2004. Yet again I was left eating humble pie when Westmeath shocked the Dubs in this year's Leinster Championship. Everyone was gunning for Tommy Lyons. He did get an unexpected phone call later that evening from the world's leading film-maker, Stephen Spielberg. Having heard about Ciaran Whelan's performance in the match he wanted to cast him in his next film, *The Invisible Man*.

Is Silence Golden?

Managers are definitely selected for winning matches rather than for the quality of their post-match interviews. They have no obligation to produce either profundity or entertainment for the microphones and notebooks that cluster round them in the half-time interval. Yet when he first became Dublin manager, Tommy proceeded to do just that.

After Dublin's defeat by Armagh in 2003, Tommy appeared to take a vow of silence. For a man who had been virtually omnipresent in the media in previous years, his sudden aversion to publicity was startling. Around this time Tommy rang Mick O'Dwyer and told him that he had just been invited by his old school to tell them all that he knew about football. He asked O'Dwyer what he should say. O'Dwyer replied, 'Tell them you've got flu.'

In my era, all the Kerry players were media-friendly. O'Dwyer always reminded us that the team–media relationship was a two-way process, and that the media were there to be used and abused. He was a past master of how to play the media and throw meat to the lions. He wouldn't say anything provocative, yet he was able to keep everybody happy. We basically adopted a poor mouth policy. The poor mouth is a religion in Kerry.

I think it is a farcical situation that managers today impose media bans on players where they aren't allowed to talk to the media. It actually adds to the pressure on the player, because when the phone rings or there's a knock on the door, the player has to say, 'I'm not here.' He ends up as a recluse.

I generally think that a lot of media bans are in place because managers want to be the head honcho. They don't want one of their players stealing the limelight. GAA players today are generally intelligent and articulate and none of them are likely to anything stupid. I think Tommy's decision to go silent before the Westmeath game was a mistake.

Tommy had decided before the game not to announce the team. The problem was that by not announcing the team, he only intensified the pressure on his players. His move backfired because everyone was speculating and asking what was going on with regard to team selection. Rather than taking heat off the players, it only added to it.

I am a complete disbeliever in that kind of mind game. In my time, Mick O'Dwyer named his 15 in the position they were actually going to line out in. Effectively he was saying to the opposition: this is our team, beat us if you can.

I genuinely believe that when you decide to play these mind games it is not the opposition you unsettle but your own team, and when you are focusing on fooling the opposition, you are not focusing on your own game. It is an admission of weakness.

The straw that broke the camel's back, though, for Tommy was his decision to leave Barry Cahill on Dessie Dolan, particularly when Barry was just coming back from serious injury. Clearly a big factor in the defeat was Dublin's failure to make positional switches.

There is a fine line between success and failure. Páidí Ó Sé brought on David Mitchell against Dublin. Mitchell is a full-back and he played him as centre-forward. It worked. If it didn't work, Páidí would have been the villain.

Sometimes to do nothing is the best choice on the sideline, but generally it is not. The good manager knows which is which. Tommy Lyons's failure to respond to the Dessie Dolan situation left him vulnerable to fans, critics and former players. And boy did they respond with a vengeance.

Backlash

The genuine Dublin fan is a great Dub, but the 'olé, olé brigade' who started following Dublin in 2002 are not. They bring the worst of soccer habits to the GAA. True fans don't humiliate their manager and players, or spit at them. I thought it was scandalous the way Tommy and the players were treated. What I found particularly shocking was that one of the people photographed berating Tommy the most forcefully was a brother of one of the players on the squad. Another interesting thing about the photo was that there was a young boy caught in the middle and the fear in his eyes was incredible. That should not happen in Gaelic football. Kerry fans don't react to defeat in the same way. They generally just sulk.

Dublin's defeat to Westmeath unleashed such a flood of media articles that half the rainforests in the Amazon must have been felled to produce the paper for all the column inches. We live in a small country. The community of GAA writers is very small, and as a result, they are all very familiar with the players and managers. When there is a need for criticism and it doesn't come, it is usually down to friendship. When there is scathing criticism in an article, it is usually because there is an agenda or because there are scores to be settled. Ex-Dublin players are not always the best people to give a ruthlessly objective view of the shortcomings of the Dublin team. In some of the most critical articles there was no mention of the fact that it was the players on the pitch who didn't deliver.

People say to me, 'Ah sure, you criticise players for their performances.' That is true and I know these guys are amateurs, but when you go on the public stage to perform, whether it is on the county football team or a role in the local drama production, you expose yourself to public scrutiny and criticism. My criticism, though, is always on the performance and is never personal. Obviously some people do take it personally, but I never mean it that way.

I always believe that it is way too easy to just blame the manager when a team loses badly. A non-playing manager has never scored a point in an All-Ireland final. But who else must share the blame for the problems in Dublin football like the lack of a decent free-taker? I believe the clubs must take some responsibility. I think we should learn from soccer in the big cities and we shouldn't just have clubs in parishes, but also in housing estates. The problem at the moment is that the dominant traditional clubs are feathering their nests. I know of a case in west Dublin where a juvenile club was set up on the borders of a club with a population of up to 200,000 people in its hinterland, and the big club has done everything in its power to stop the juvenile club from developing. It is scandalous. There should be five times the numbers of GAA clubs in the county which would provide a much bigger pool of home-grown talent. The problem is exacerbated by the fact that many clubs are being very short-sighted by parachuting in players from outside while promising home-grown youngsters are left on the sideline.

It was totally unfair to make Tommy Lyons the scapegoat for all of the problems of Dublin football. The level of personal criticism aimed at Tommy was way over the top. He was not the only one in that situation, however. Joe Brolly was very, very critical of Mickey Moran before and after Derry's defeat by Tyrone. I know Mickey Moran rang the powers that be in RTÉ and complained about the nature of the criticism that was levelled at him. He made the valid point that he was watching it on the television with his 15-year-old daughter. It would be as tough on anyone in that position.

The day after the Dublin–Westmeath match, a friend of mine went to the doctor because he was getting chest pains. The doctor told him that he had too much stress in his life and needed to reduce the stress points in his life.

My friend asked, 'How do I do that?'

The doctor replied, 'Avoid excitement. Watch the Dubs.'

As he is a good friend of mine, I rang Tommy the day after the defeat and advised him that it was better for him to come out with all guns blazing and not to run away from his critics. I cited two examples of people who had found themselves in sticky situations who had come out and admitted they had made errors in judgement, namely Ben Dunne and his 'incident' in Florida, and Emmet Stagg TD and his 'episode' in the Phoenix Park. I said to Tommy, 'Come out, hold your hands up and admit you made mistakes.'

The only suitable replacement for Tommy I can think of that could live up to the aspirations of Dublin fans is Merlin the Magician. Tommy did take remedial reaction afterwards, however, such as recalling Dessie Farrell to the Dublin panel. I enjoyed Dessie's comment about one of his team-mates: 'The opposition are much more dangerous when he has the ball.'

Tommy did get three lucky breaks in the draw for the back-door games with London, Leitrim and Longford, which gave Dublin the opportunity for gentle rehabilitation. They were also lucky to draw Roscommon, though if Roscommon had shown more composure in front of goal they would have beaten them.

I met Tommy in Jury's Hotel on the Saturday night after Dublin lost to Westmeath. They had just beaten London. Tommy was far more relaxed. The great thing was that the 'olé, olé brigade' didn't arrive at the match, and the team in general, and Tommy in particular, got a great welcome. The Dublin players were in the bar as well. I don't enjoy that sort of a situation as I don't like to get too close to players in case it compromises my objectivity and colours my opinion. I would like to think that if I was watching my brother playing in a match, I would call it as I saw it, without fear or favour.

That night I had gone out to get advance copies of the Sunday papers. I had written a sympathetic article about Tommy in my column, but I hadn't written the headline. I nearly fell off my chair when I read it: 'Jackeens like Jack-asses!' To compound my discomfort, the Dublin-midfielder, Darren Homan, asked me what I had written about them in my column. That was the moment I decided to sprint out of the bar! I only stopped to tell Tommy Lyons's wife, Noreen, that I had not written the headline for my column.

The following night on *The Sunday Game*, I asked Colm O'Rourke to clarify comments he had made within minutes of Dublin's defeat to Westmeath when it seemed as if he had been calling for Tommy's resignation. Colm clearly explained that if he had been in Tommy's position, he would have resigned immediately after the loss to Westmeath, anticipating the inevitable backlash and mindful of the strain it was going to put on Tommy's family. Tommy rang me the next morning to tell me that he had got 25 texts telling him that I had put Colm O'Rourke on the spot. Yet another reminder, not that I needed one, that television is all about perception.

Even some of the production team on the programme were concerned afterwards that I had put Colm on the spot, but I think Colm was glad to put his position on the record because he felt he had been accused in the wrong. Tommy Lyons was very appreciative of his clarification. I said to him, 'You have one enemy to cross off your list.'

There has been a plus side to Dublin's defeat by Westmeath, however. In darkest Africa there was a river infested with crocodiles. On the other side there was a tribe which various missionaries wanted to convert. However, nobody was willing to take the risk of crossing the river. In 2004, along came a group of Irish priests who waded across the river without coming to any harm. Shortly after they revealed their secret. 'We wore T-shirts bearing the words "Dublin, All-Ireland Champions, 2004". And sure not even a crocodile was willing to swallow that!'

Tommy saw the writing on the wall and stepped down in September. I liked the fact that he retained his sense of humour throughout. This was particularly evident when he took the journalists at his press conference by surprise when he began by saying that he was there to announce that he had got a three-year extension to his contract!

Knock, Knock, Knockin' on Heaven's Door

After Dublin's shock defeat by Westmeath in the quarter-final of the Leinster Championship, a new story started to do the rounds. Three elderly men, one from Galway, one from Cork and one from Dublin go into a Church to seek God's help by asking him who would do what and when.

The Galway man asks, 'When will Galway win the All-Ireland?'

A voice booms down from heaven: 'In eight years.'

The Galway man shakes his head sadly and says, 'I'll be dead by then'.

The Cork chap is next and he asks, 'When will Cork win the All-Ireland?'

A voice booms down from heaven: 'In 12 years.'

The Cork man shakes his head sadly and says, 'I'll be dead by then'.

The Dub asks, 'When will Dublin win the All-Ireland?'

God's voice booms down from heaven: '*I'll* be dead by then.'

13

Where They Sported and Played

In Cork at the very mention of my name they all burst into song. Mind you, the song they sing is 'The Langer'!

When people think of the great Kerry team of the 1970s and 1980s, they automatically assume that our greatest rivals were Dublin. However, Cork generally pushed us to the pin of our collar. I gave a talk in January 2004 at the Jury's Sportstar of the Year awards. Talk about meeting the enemies! Niall Cahalane was in the audience. He was probably the most difficult player I ever marked. I told the crowd that Niall had such a love of the Kerry jersey that he used to collect bits and pieces of my jersey while marking me so closely all through the years.

I was thinking of Niall during the Leinster semifinal between Laois and Meath this year. I thought if I had worn the same sort of figure-hugging jersey the Laois boys were wearing that day, Niall wouldn't have been able to catch hold of me. I can't see those jerseys becoming a big hit with Junior B club football teams. They would not project the bellies of your typical players on those sides in the most flattering light.

My worst Cork memory, though, was not during a football match, but at my first after-dinner speech, in UCC rugby club. I was all excited when I got there. I should have been worried. The previous year, the speaker had been Moss Keane. Big Moss is a legend in UCC, but the students gave him a hard time, so I should have known the writing was on the wall. I was making my debut on the after-dinner circuit – surely a passport to big bucks. I was doing it for a friend, a doctor in Cork. We went to a pre-dinner reception which was kindly sponsored by a drinks company. I drank a lot of pints. My wife came with me and she was all set for a great night. I started my speech. It was going well. The students, however, got restless very quickly. I kept talking … must finish my speech. The students were getting even more restless … more gags to go … I must finish my speech. I was dying a death. I was determined to finish when I noticed that even the people on the table alongside me were talking. In a drunken haze I turned to the man beside me and said, 'Excuse me, sir. If you want to talk, you come up here and talk.' It didn't go down well. How was I to know that he was the local District Court judge? Bad speech. My wife didn't talk to me for two days and she hasn't come to one of my after-dinner speeches since. Lesson learned!

Fit for Nothing

It was the Cork team who effectively signed the death sentence for the great Kerry team when they beat us in 1987. Everyone thought Kerry and Dublin were the dominant teams in the 1970s and 1980s because of frightening physical regimes. This was actually incorrect, but it was a good rumour to throw out at the time. Everyone aped us with the result that fellas with no knowledge of football, who earned a great living training teams at intercounty level, and even more worryingly at club level, drove players into the ground by making them run incessantly. When people heard about these tough regimes, they said knowingly: 'Isn't he a mighty man.' But two things happened as a consequence. First, the standard of football dropped alarmingly because we were producing athletes and runners rather than footballers. The second thing is that these men are responsible for the huge number of crocked ex-players who are the result of that intensive training from these years.

Today fitness gurus are all the rage. When the iron man from Rhode, Paddy McCormack, was training Offaly for a year, his style of training was laps, laps and more laps. Eventually the players said to him, 'We're sick to the death of all these laps. Tonight we want something different.'

Paddy thought for a moment and said, 'Okay, lads, that's fine. Turn around and run the other way for a change.'

Still the mantra today is fitness, fitness, fitness. You're supposed to be below a certain percentage of body fat, fit in with a certain body profile, pass the bleep test, and you are supposed to be able to do a certain amount of shuttle runs within a certain time. As a result, we are producing athletes who can't kick the ball. One man who does not fit into the profile is Geoffrey McConigle. Joe Brolly compared the shape of Geoffrey's bum to two bags of cement. Yet I noted that in the first game of the League this year he scored six points and in the second game he scored eight.

A Corker

I attribute much of Cork's success in the late 1980s and early 1990s to Billy Morgan. He brought a very professional approach which involved drawing on the expertise of other experts.

Bitter experience has taught me the value of having a proper back-up team in place. In my playing days, I was one of the many players who made trips to America to play in the New York championship. It was an ideal opportunity to make a few dollars and have a holiday. Big name stars over from Ireland were always subject to 'robust' play on the field. On one occasion this necessitated me visiting the medical room with blood pouring from my nose. The Italian doctor who was on duty was more interested in reading *The New York Times* than attending to me. Without looking up from his paper he asked me what was wrong. I said, 'I think I've broken my nose.' With no concern in his voice, the doctor told me to go over to the mirror and clean off the blood. When this task was completed he inquired, 'Does it look different than it did this morning?' I replied, 'Yes, it's crooked.' The doctor calmly mused, 'You probably broke your nose then.' Thus ended the medical consultation.

Mind Over Matter

Managers play all kinds of mind games.

Two years ago, the then Donegal coach, John Morrison, apparently gave all his players a nut. It was to remind them of Brazil and the skill and quality of their football team.

In Billy Morgan's first incarnation as manager of Cork he allegedy employed two psychologists to get the team in the right frame of mind before playing a Munster final against Kerry. The first guy had the job of calming the team down. Everyone had to close their eyes and picture themselves walking along a river bank on a summer's evening while butterflies fluttered around them. There was the smell of freshly mown grass and the sounds of birds singing nearby. The players then had to imagine walking up a little path on a hill to a cabin, entering into the cabin, sitting down and feeling at peace. I've always imagined how a player like Niall Cahalane, who would always be really pumped up for a big match like that, would have reacted to such an exercise.

The second psychologist had the job of getting the team all fired up, ready to play out of their skins when they got out on the pitch. The Cork team left the dressing-room to the sound of Tina Turner singing 'Simply the Best' ringing in their ears. What happened? Kerry hammered the living daylights out of them that year.

Billy's innovative methods did not always get the response he was hoping for. Another year, after Linford Christie won the gold medal in the Olympics, the mantra in the Cork dressing-room was that the Cork team should take inspiration from him. For ten minutes the team had the virtues of Linford extolled to them.

When the inspirational words were finished, a very prominent Cork player, a household name, turned to another and whispered, in all sincerity, in a bewildered tone: 'Who the f**k is Linford Christie?'

Mind you, not all great motivational tactics backfire in the dressing-room. Sometimes the manager can say exactly the right thing. In the 1995 Munster hurling final, when Clare trailed Cork by four points and faced the wind in the second half, Ger Loughnane defiantly told his team, 'The ship has sprung a leak but we are not going down!' They didn't.

Half-time speeches can backfire just as easily, though. When he was Tipperary hurling manager, Babs Keating faced the problem of rallying his team even though they were trailing at half-time by eight points. After a number of inspirational words in an effort to instil confidence, he went around the team individually and asked each of them, 'Can we do it?'

To a man they replied, 'We can. We can.'

He could feel the surge of belief invading the dressing-room. Everything was going swimmingly until he turned to Joe Hayes and asked, 'Joe, can we do it?'

Joe replied, 'It's not looking great is it, Babs?'

Babs has a history of putting his foot in his mouth. In 1990, Cork were given no chance of winning the Munster hurling final against All-Ireland champions, Tipperary. A chance comment from Babs before the game that 'donkeys don't win derbies' galvanised the Cork team and the Leesiders claimed victory.

In the build-up to one of the early rounds of the Ulster Championship this year, one of the northern managers came up with an unusual motivational strategy. He put two planks across a skip and got each of his players to stand on them. One of the team's mentors told the players that if they fell off the planks they would be rubbish and if they lost the match they would be rubbish. Did it work? No. They lost tamely.

The most effective motivation comes from within. Mick O'Dwyer's half-time speeches were always inspirational as they always came from the heart. His speech was basically the same each time and after 13 years we had heard it all before. O'Dwyer was giving us a pep talk before one of our All-Irelands and his false teeth fell out, but we were all so pysched up that none of us noticed it! It wasn't until one of the subs mentioned it afterwards that we became aware of it. We were in the zone.

As Unhappy as Larry

It is a great tribute to Billy Morgan that when Kerry played Cork in the Munster semifinal earlier this year, Kerry fans were worried, not because of any of the Cork players, but because of the admiration they had for Morgan's record against Kerry down the years. Their fears were totally unjustified as Cork had little to offer. Watching the game I was thinking of Ireland's abysmal performance in the Eurovision Song Contest this year. Specifically I was thinking of the joke that was doing the rounds then that Chris Doran drove from Waterford to Dublin at 100 mph. He was frantically trying to get two points. Cork's play that day looked just as desperate.

Talking to Cork fans afterwards, the only consolation they had was that, as they saw it, at least Larry Tompkins was no longer in charge of the team. Larry was a great player, but getting a Cork fan to say something nice about his time as Cork manager is as difficult as pushing custard up a hill.

Larry is a lovely fella and a gentleman. He was probably the first professional Gaelic footballer – not in the sense that he was getting paid, but because he trained morning, noon and night, seven days a week. He devoted his entire life to it. The problem was, despite the fact that he captained Cork to an All-Ireland in 1990, people in Cork still, to this day, think of him as a 'blow-in', which means he was only grudgingly accepted.

The failing that Larry had as a manager was that he tried to train the team to be like him, to be as dedicated, determined and fanatical about fitness as he was. He had them running up hills. He brought them to beaches for early morning runs. Eugene McGee was the first to do this with UCD. Ger Loughnane did it with the Clare hurlers. Since the ploy failed for Larry, no other team have used it. Larry's man-management skills were also poor. Knowing that things were looking bleak for their All-Ireland prospects in his final year in charge, Larry rang Joe Kernan and asked, 'What's the recipe for winning an All-Ireland final?'

Big Joe replied, 'You get the following drill: get loads of cones, place them carefully around the field, get loads of balls, have the players soloing around the cones, doing one-twos, side-steps, swerves, and kick the ball over the bar.'

After a few weeks Joe was surprised that Larry hadn't rang him to thank him for his brilliant advice, so he rang Tompkins and asked him how well they'd get on. Larry replied, 'Not great. The cones beat us by six points.'

Finding Nemo

After Larry, Billy Morgan was expected to be the second coming of the Messiah for Cork, but it did not work out that way. Cork's fall from grace has been gathering momentum from some time. There are three main reasons for this. First, the standard of club football in Cork is very poor. The best midfielder in last year's Championship was 40-year-old Niall Cahalane – enough said. Nemo Rangers have dominated Cork football for years. They play to a particular system, but once they are taken out of that system and handed a county jersey, they look very ordinary. Second, there are far too many GAA officials in Cork who are so focused on the rule book, pre-occupied with outdated ideologies and so narrow-minded in their outlook that they have lost sight of the bigger picture. Third, hurling is the number-one game in the country and football has to settle for second best.

Any time I have ever been asked to choose my greatest Gaelic football team of all time, Billy Morgan has always been my automatic choice for goalkeeper. He was a great reader of the game, superb organiser of defenders, inspirational leader and had excellent reflexes, and he brought all of these qualities to the manager's job. His leadership and motivation is second to none. He will probably rank as one of the greatest club managers of all time with Nemo Rangers. I have heard it said that he would die for Nemo, but would only get wounded for Cork. He can have a short fuse and you wouldn't want to be around him then, but he remains a real gentleman.

The Cork County Board seems to favour austere personalities. It is interesting to note that, in 2002, they appointed Donal O'Grady as their hurling manager. I enjoyed Keith Duggan's comment in *The Irish Times* in September 2003: 'When Donal O'Grady smiles you can hear the cello in *Jaws*.'

In that context I had a fascinating conversation with Brian Corcoran during the summer. Brian returned to the inter-county scene after a break for a couple of years, and it showed me just how professional Gaelic games has become. He told me that when they came into training, their gear was up on a hook for them. All they needed to bring in were their boots and their hurleys. After the training was over, they just left their gear behind them and someone washed it for them. In terms of fitness, Brian said that the drills that were in vogue three years ago are now considered obsolete. The biggest change he found, though, was that when the manager comes into training now, he brings his laptop and can pull out clips from any of the Cork games. That sums up the modern game in a nutshell, but whether its good or bad for the game is debatable.

Old Rivals

In my time, Cork and Kerry players always enjoyed an intense but generally good-natured rivalry. To fully understand the rivalry in my playing days we had to look to Ambrose O'Donovan. His farm in Gneevguila straddled the Cork–Kerry border. He is a lovely guy, but when we played Cork, it was like he had transformed into *The Incredible Hulk*. He had an absolute hatred of losing to Cork. His attitude was if we beat them in the Munster final, that would keep them quiet for 12 months. When Kerry lose to Cork in the Munster Championship the Cork fans will stay in Kenmare all night. When Cork lose, they drive straight through Kenmare at 5.30 that evening as fast as they can.

One of Cork's stars when they regained the All-Ireland in 1989 was John Cleary – a very accurate forward, though not the biggest man in the world. Before one of Cork's clashes with Kerry, Jack O'Shea came up to him, and in an effort to psyche him out, said, 'You're too small and too young for a game like this.' Cleary said nothing until after the game when Cork emerged triumphant. As he walked off the pitch past Jacko he softly replied, 'You're too old for a game like this.'

Kerry remain the undisputed kings of Gaelic football, however. In 2002, Kerry and Cork figured in an historic all Munster All-Ireland semifinal. The Kerry manager Páidí Ó Sé asked for a home match for Kerry. Cork generously did not object, so the match was played in Croke Park.

Cork fans enjoy nothing more than slagging off the Kerry team whenever the opportunity presents itself. In January 2003, Páidí Ó Sé got embroiled in a major controversy when he described the Kerry fans as 'f***ing animals'. One Cork fan suggested immediately that Kerry's nickname should no longer be 'the kingdom' but 'the animal kingdom'. Another suggested that in future, Cork should play all their home games against Kerry in Fota Wildlife Park to make the Kerry fans feel at home.

Yet a further joke was that they were putting animal grids on the Cork county borders to prevent the animals from crossing over.

Sadly we lost one of our great Kerry champions at putting Cork people in their place with the death of John B. Keane. He could pour scorn on their intelligence: 'Cork footballers think oral sex is just talking about it.' He also joked about their tactical *nous*: 'A typical piece of advice from a Cork manager is: keep your high balls low into the wind.'

In the glory days of the Kerry team, John B. told the story of a match when Cork trailed Kerry by 2–19 to 0–5 at half-time. Kerry were to play with a gale force wind in the second half. So desperate were the Cork mentors in the dressing-room at half-time that they asked the tea lady if she had any advice for them. After pausing for thought, she said, 'If ye want to prolong yer stay in the Championship the only thing ye can do is stay as long as ye possibly can here in the dressing-room.'

Them and Us

Who has the most loyal supporters? There has always been a great rivalry between Cork and Kerry fans. A Kerry fan goes up to heaven and he is very surprised to see that Saint Peter is wearing a Cork jersey. 'Why should I let you in here?' asked Saint Peter.

The Kerry fan replied, 'Well last month I gave €100 to the Vincent de Paul. Last week I gave €60 to Focus Ireland. Yesterday I gave €40 to Trócaire.'

Saint Peter replied, 'I'm not sure if we want a Kerry fan in Heaven, but seeing as you gave generously to charity, wait here and I'll check out with God what he thinks of your situation.'

Saint Peter came back a few minutes later and said, 'God agrees with me. Here's your €200. Now f**k off out of here.'

Of course Cork fans have a few stories about my good self. They tell the story that when I go to the airport and the security ask whether I have any sharp objects, I reply, 'Only my tongue.'

They also cryptically say that I'm the guy who put the 'tit' into 'titterer'.

In reality, though, they think very highly of me in Cork which is why *The Examiner* printed the following story about me. It is based on my fictitious sister, Daphne, who is heavily pregnant and rushed into hospital. After giving birth she falls unconscious but wakes up, days later, to discover she has had twins, a boy and a girl. She is thrilled to discover this news until she finds out that I have christened them on her behalf. The blood drains from her face. When she regains her composure she says, in a voice breaking with emotion, 'How could you let him do that? Don't you know he hasn't got an ounce of brains in his thick head. What did he call the girl?'

'Deniece,' the nurse replies.

'Really? Denise is a lovely name. I didn't think he had it in him to come up with a wonderful name like that. I'm thrilled with his choice. So what did he call my lovely boy?'

'Denephew.'

14

Into the West

Football supporters are creatures of habit. This brings its own pitfalls. A former Mayo footballer died as a result of a massive heart attack. His granddaughter visited his wife and asked what happened. The grandmother said, 'Last Sunday morning we made love and your grandfather suffered a heart attack and died.'

The granddaughter asked, 'Don't you think shagging at 94 is dangerous?'

The grandmother shook her head and said, 'Oh no, every Sunday morning we made love in time with the church bells: in with the ding, out with the dong and only for that ice-cream van that passed by he would still be alive.'

One habit that football fans have in Connacht is slagging me off. A typical example of this was a Sligo fan's summation of my football career: 'Pat Spillane had the speed of a racehorse, the strength of a plough horse and the brains of a rocking horse.'

While I get a large volume of hate mail, from time to time I get correspondence that suggests that there are people out there who understand that my frequent criticism of Connacht football is not malicious. In July 2002, after I had slagged off the Sligo team, though, they had a great run in the Championship and shocked Tyrone in Croke Park and pushed Armagh all the way. I got the following poem from Padraic Neary, which brought a smile to my face.

Poor Pat

Poor Pat Spillane can't carry on, his face is green and sickly,
His heartbeat's slow, his pulse is low, oh get a doctor quickly.
His only cure, is a jab for sure, preferably in the rectum,
That Sligo crew, don't have a clue, how badly they affect him.

His life's in a mess, he can hardly dress, his sweaty hands are shaking,
He can't guess what's wrong, as he shuffles along, every nerve and bone is
   aching.
His job's in peril at the Sunday World, though Pat's not really lazy,
He just can't write, in black and white, the colours drive him crazy.

On a Dublin street, he chanced to meet, a Meath man of great learning,
'O'Rourke,' says Pat, 'I'm feeling cat, my throat is raw and burning.
It's the cursed sight of the black and white, that's left me turned and
   tossing',
And with no other sound, he fell to the ground, in a heap on a zebra
   crossing.

One day last week, Pat was asked to speak, on some TV sports discussions,
The Producer swore, if she knew the score, she'd have cancelled and sod the
   repercussions.
Everything went fine, till a faulty camera nine, faded colour from the TVs
   of the nation,
At the sudden sight, of himself in black and white, he went berserk and
   demolished half the station.

Things came to a head, when one night in bed, as he tried to sleep even
   harder,
His wife, poor thing, was just trying to bring, some passion back to his
   ardour,
How could she know, that his mind would go, why, to her he was God
   almighty,
But his lid he flipped, when she suddenly slipped, into a short black
   nightie.

Galway Boys Hurrah

'Nothing is permanent but change.' So said Heraclitus, Greek philosopher, 500 BC. I spent the first seven years of my career as a pundit slagging off Connacht football. When John O'Mahony led Galway to the All-Ireland in 1998, I was forced to sing a new tune. However, I was very critical again of Galway in 2000 for letting the All-Ireland title slip from their grasp. Then their All-Ireland title in 2001 saw me backtracking faster than Michael Schumacher in reverse.

After seven years at the top, John O'Mahony resigned as Galway manager after they lost to Tyrone in the Qualifiers. He is a very astute, shrewd manager who is most meticulous in his preparation. John always had excellent video analysis for his team before games.

The great managers are often not easy men. They have to be driven by an endless quest to avoid the inevitable, to minimise risks and to maximise potential. Management is a process of replacing one anxiety with another. O'Mahony is noted for his attention to detail. You can never leave anything to chance if you want to be successful. In 2002, the Irish rugby team visited Siberia to play a match in an area renowned for its freezing temperatures. As the players are a very pampered lot, they can normally get everything they need. On this trip, incredibly they found there was one thing they couldn't get – ice cubes! I bet if John O'Mahony was in charge, the ice cubes would be there.

After taking Mayo to the All-Ireland final in 1989, the Mayo County Board were criticised by many for the way they got rid of John. If they had kept faith in him, by now they would have the All-Ireland they have craved for 53 years.

One of the main reasons why Connacht teams generally struggled so badly in Croke Park in the 1980s and early 1990s was a lack of top-class forwards. In recent times Galway have had two of the top forwards in the game in Padraic Joyce and Michael Donnellan.

Joyce is one of the most accurate kickers of the ball in the game. One thing I've always found strange is the way commentators refer to players like him as having a 'cultured left foot'. Why is that they never speak of having a cultured right foot? Joyce had a poor year in 2003. He wasn't fully fit and seemed to have lost his appetite for the game, but this year he was back to his brilliant best.

Michael Donnellan is one of the great enigmas of Gaelic football, capable of going from hero to zero in the one game. One of the great sights in Gaelic football is seeing Michael Donnellan gathering the ball in defence, soloing up the field, and getting a great point or more, particularly with one of his trademark goals. People will long recall his great goal against Kerry in the All-Ireland final in 2002, to take just one example. If he has problems it is that there seems to have been a difficult relationship between him and John O'Mahony. I often think that had Mick O'Dwyer, with his famed man-management skills, been in charge of him, he would have gone on to be one of the greatest players of all time. Now that John has stepped down, a lot of these underachieving Galway players will have no excuse next year, and if there is any blame going around, they will finally have to take their fair share.

Lovely Leitrim

Leitrim teams have generally struggled on the national stage with devastating consequences. Persistent heavy defeat drains the confidence of a team and requires some imaginative motivational ploys to overcome. A club team from Leitrim travelled 200 miles to a tournament game in Waterford. At half-time they trailed by 7–2 to 0–5, and a crisis meeting was held in the middle of the pitch. Recriminations were flying until the captain called for silence and an end to the bickering, and a hush descended.

One player said, 'We need some positive encouragement.'

After a short silence, the manager-cum-trainer-cum-club secretary-cum-groundskeeper said, 'Come on now lads. Let's go out there and show them up. It's plain to be seen, they can't score points!'

Leitrim did very well to draw against Roscommon in this year's Connacht Championship. They were right there in the game until the second period of the second half of the replay, but it wasn't a major surprise when Roscommon pulled away in the end. One big surprise, however, was related to me after the match by a former Leitrim player who explained that the comic book heroes held their annual convention in Carrick-on-Shannon. Superman was late and when he arrived he met the Incredible Hulk who asked, 'Superman, what's after happening to you?'

His cape was torn, there was blood pouring from his nose, he had a black eye and he was bedraggled.

Superman said, 'I was flying in low coming to the party and when I looked down who did I spy down by the banks of the Shannon but Wonderwoman – naked.'

'I suppose you couldn't resist the temptation and you went in for the kill.'

'You bet.'

'She must have got a big surprise.'

'Not half as big as the Invisible Man!'

As the Leitrim team has not had so many opportunities to perform on national television, I have thankfully managed not to annoy Leitrim people too much. I think I got a few brownie points, a very rare occurrence, when, after John O'Mahony guided them to only their second Connacht title in 1994 after they beat Mayo in the Connacht final, I said, 'Leitrim for Croke Park. Mayo for Croagh Patrick.'

The Rossies

They are much tougher on me in Roscommon than the nice people of Leitrim. They have incredible memories in Roscommon and have never forgotten, not to mention forgiven, my 'performance' in the 1980 All-Ireland. Mind you I wonder if it is a case of the pot calling the kettle black. In the Connacht final in 2001, Roscommon's Frankie Dolan was perceived by some Mayo fans as engaging in 'theatricals' which 'caused' a Mayo player to be sent off. They gave him a new nickname: 'Frankie goes to Hollywood.'

I was delighted to be chosen on Gaelic football's team of the millennium. Like the rest of the team my image was commemorated on a special stamp. When it arrived in post offices in Roscommon, nobody was sure which side they should spit on.

Tommy Carr brought new discipline to the Rossies when he became their manager. It was badly needed. Two Roscommon players talent for playing pool in the nude made headlines in 2002. When a second major breach of discipline occurred that summer, the Roscommon County Board decided to disband the entire county panel. Given the penchant for nude pool among his senior county players, Tom Mullaney, Secretary of the Roscommon County Board, showed a flair for double entendre in his appraisal of the disciplinary measures: 'As a group, all players hang together or hang separately.'

Writing in *The Irish Times*, Keith Duggan's verdict on that Roscommon policy of 'total disclosure' when playing pool made for amusing reading:

> *Ah yes, the career of the Gaelic footballer can end in a flash.*
> *Just ask any of the Roscommon senior players. It will take*
> *many, many years before a Roscommon senior manager can*
> *stand before his team in the dressing-room and bellow the*
> *traditional GAA rallying cry, 'Show them yez have the balls*
> *for it lads'.*

It seems to have been forgotten by most people that Tommy Carr began his career as a footballer with Tipperary. It is something he doesn't like to be reminded of! In a way he is quite similar in character to his friend John Maughan, because fitness and discipline seem to be the hallmarks of his managerial style. The fact that both have an army background may have something to do with it. Like Maughan, I think Tommy has mellowed in recent years and that he has improved his man-management skills and become sharper tactically and more astute in his switches from the sideline.

He got very close to the Holy Grail as Dublin manager, but I believe he got an incredibly raw deal from the Dublin County Board who shafted him. There is no other word for it. I think he did well with Roscommon in 2003, but that's probably as far as he can ever go with them.

Roscommon had all the hallmarks of an over-trained team in this year's Connacht final, but they redeemed themselves somewhat with their display against Dublin. Tommy Carr took a very bold decision to drop two of his star players, Frankie Dolan and Karol Mannion, for that match. I can not remember when any manager made such a decision before his team's biggest game of the year in Croke Park. He certainly got a good performance out of the Rossies and had they either a Tony McManus in the forwards to put away the chances they created or a rock-like defender such as Harry Keegan to thwart the Dublin attack, they would have won that match.

My scathing comments about the Roscommon forward line down the years have not gone unpunished throughout the county. A story was related about me on Shannonside Radio, recalling a visit I had to my home from Mick O'Dwyer. As I was getting so much hate mail at the time from disgruntled Roscommon fans, I had acquired two new dogs for protection. Micko asked me what their names were. I responded by saying that one was named 'Rolex' and the other was named 'Timex'.

Dwyer asked, 'Whoever heard of someone naming dogs like that?'

'Hello?' I answered. 'They're watch dogs!'

A Cold Wind from the West

This summer has provided me with a *déjà vu* experience. After seven years of virtual silence I am being publicly vilified again in Mayo. It was like old times in September when I received a big article by Toni Bourke in the *Connacht Telegraph*. The headline told me what was in store: 'P*at Spillane, the biggest anti-Mayo man.' Toni, come on out and just call me a 'prat'. Mayo football fans were calling me a lot worse than that in 1996 and 1997. Toni's article then began by saying that his joy at Mayo's victory over Fermanagh was 'quickly deflated' after he read my column. He went on: 'My blood never boiled as much after reading a match review as it did after reading Pat Spillane's comments in the *Sunday World*. What did the people of Mayo ever do to make him hate us, our football team and out style of football so much? Usually I would disregard any anti-Mayo sentiments coming from that has-been but last Sunday morning he got my shackles up.'

By the way Toni, thanks for your joke about the Kerry–Derry semifinal: 'P*at, the real reason there were so few Kerry people at the game on Sunday was because they were at home watching their (mad priest) man in the Olympics. Hee, hee, hee.' Hilarious.

Apparently my comments were 'blinkered' by my 'incessant condemnation of Mayo football'. Let me set the record straight. First, the team I have criticised most in the Championship has not been Mayo by a long shot, but my beloved Kerry for not playing 'the Kerry way'. Second, my article reflected what I have said about Mayo for most of the year. This is what I wrote on that day that I so offended Mayo sensibilities:

Maughan's men started out far more like the boys that had sent Galway, Roscommon and Tyrone spinning out of the All-Ireland Championship. Their attacking movement was excellent, whether a Mayo half-back or midfielder got the ball, there were options ahead of him, there was always a man running into space. Conor Mortimer and Kieran McDonald were excellent. The latter spread the ball around beautifully for Mayo, the former finished off the moves with a point. Fermanagh could not get this Mortimer marked at all in the first half.

I know I am not the brightest in the world, but this does not sound like 'incessant criticism' to me.

Any critical comments I made of the Mayo–Fermanagh replay was essentially designed to highlight the fact that the fairytale success of Westmeath and Fermanagh distracted attention from a serious analysis of the quality of the football this year. While there was a lot of excitement and entertainment, the quality of the fare on offer left a lot to be desired. What makes this all the more galling is that more time and effort are being put into the preparation of teams than ever before, yet we are not getting even better games or higher skill levels. The Championship provided us with one hell of a rollercoaster ride. There were shocks, surprises and close contests but we got our excitement at the expense of quality.

For the record, early this summer I was invited to appear on the popular UTV GAA series *End to End*. I was asked who my dark horse for the All-Ireland was. When I replied Mayo, one of the presenters was incredulous, but I felt that they had the potential to go far with their potent cocktail of youth and talent. Above all, Maughan's men have what Mayo football was missing for so long, quality forwards who could score.

In my article, I had said that the standard of the Mayo–Fermanagh game was like that of a Junior B match. Rather than ranting about me, Mayo people might have been better served listening to the warning bells in my comments. Although they were the fairytale team, Fermanagh were an ordinary side and Mayo's shortcomings were painfully exposed in the All-Ireland final.

The Green and Red of Mayo

They don't like me in Roscommon, but they really hate me in Mayo! In fact, I have complained about them to Amnesty International. They have done me a grave injustice. They wrongly attribute to me a story that was doing the rounds that reflected their place in the football hierarchy before they beat Galway in this year's Connacht Championship. A young boy's parents were getting divorced. The judge asked him, 'Would you like to live with your father?'

'No, he beats me.'

'So you would like to live with your mother?'

'No, she beats me.'

'Well, who would you like to live with?'

'The Mayo football team – they can beat nobody!'

I have spoken about the many shortcomings of the Mayo forwards so often it is like I have been reciting a litany. Mind you, the Kildare forwards have given them a close run down the years with the Cavan forwards a close third.

Earlier this year, George Bush was looking to put Saddam Hussein in a place where he would never threaten anyone. So he put him in the Mayo forward line.

I am reliably informed that my face adorns many a dart board in pubs around Mayo. However, the time has come for me to confound my critics and bravely admit that in the last five years Mayo have had one of the best teams I have ever seen – their ladies football team!

In March I was watching the news at six on RTÉ television. For a second I was wondering why *Footballers Wives* was on TV two or three hours before the watershed, as there were blonde streaks, pink baseball caps, designer sunglasses and tight jeans. It was visiting time in the local prison in Spain when three Leicester players were arrested for alleged sexual assault. It was at that moment I was struck by a very rare brainwave. I can now exclusively reveal that plans are well advanced for my new series about Mayo footballers. It is to be called *Footballer's Husbands*.

Vengeance is Theirs

Of course, I could not expect my repeated rants about Mayo to go unpunished. Mayo people have targeted my golf game to cut me down to size and expose some of my many shortcomings. A story about my adventures on the fairways appeared in a match programme in Mayo. Colm O'Rourke and I were out playing golf, and we decided to put some competition into the game by putting some serious money on the round – €1. With such a sum at stake, both of us were concentrating fiercely, and we were perfectly matched for the first nine holes. On the tenth, though, I drove into the rough and couldn't find my ball. I called Colm over to help and the pair of us searched around. Finally, desperate to avoid the four-stroke penalty for a lost ball, I popped a new ball out of my pocket when Colm wasn't looking.

'Colm, I've found the ball,' I said.

'You filthy, cheating swine!' exploded Colm. 'I never thought that any friend of mine would stoop so low as to cheat in a game that had money on it.'

'I'm not cheating!' I protested. 'I've found my ball, and I'll play it where it lies.'

'That's not your ball,' snarled Colm. 'I've been standing on your ball for the last five minutes.'

15

Managers Speak

Conversation with Gaelic football managers is a very hazardous experience, because there are a lot of sensitive issues to be avoided and a lot of potential minefields. The following guide is offered to help you safely negotiate your way through your next meeting with a famous manager.

Tommy Lyons

What to say:
'You are the saviour of Dublin football.'
''Twas an awful pity Ray Cosgrove hit the post that time.'
'Your arseboxing quote is the best GAA quote of all time.'

What not to say:
'Vincents should be running Dublin football.'
'*Sportscall* listeners know their stuff.'
'Have you ever trained a county team to win an All-Ireland?'

Páidí Ó Sé

What to say:
''Twas a disgrace the way the Kerry County Board treated you. You were right about those animals.'
'Your interview in South Africa was outstanding.'
'You should stand for Fianna Fáil in South Kerry.'

What not to say:

'The Tralee boys really know their football.'

'Seamus McGearailt and John O'Keeffe were the real brains behind Kerry's successes in 1997 and 2000.'

'Sure you only went to Westmeath for the money.'

Tommy Carr

What to say:

'You were blackguarded by Dublin.'

'You will win an All-Ireland yet with the Rossies.'

'Ye were unlucky that time against Kerry.'

What not to say:

'Why did you leave Tipperary?'

'John Bailey is the greatest County Chairman of all time.'

'You are going soft, Tommy.'

Seán Boylan

What to say:

'You were great on the telly hanging with Hector.'

'There's great stuff in those syrups you use.'

'Eamon Barry should never have challenged you.'

What not to say:

'I think O'Rourke would be the man to get the job.'

'You've nothing else to give Meath.'

'The point Colm Coyle scored in 1996 was the greatest fluke of all time.'

Brian McEniff

What to say:

'I love staying in your hotels.'

'You are the greatest multi-tasker in the GAA.'

'You did an excellent job with the International Rules team.'

What not to say:

'McHugh is the saviour of Donegal football.'

'Spillane was right in his analysis of your term as International Rules manager.'

'Why were Donegal so unfit for their first round game against Fermanagh?'

'The only good thing to come out of Donegal was Daniel O'Donnell.'

John Maughan

What to say:

'What great legs you have!'

'Did you ever think of becoming a male model?'

'You are the best manager to come out of Mayo, and that includes John O'Mahony.'

'Spillane would talk a rat to death.'

What not to say:

'Are you putting on a bit of weight?'

'Why did you leave Pat Holmes on Maurice Fitzgerald for so long?'

'That Colm Coyle was a great player.'

'Liam McHale deserved to be put off that time.'

Billy Morgan

What to say:

'Only for you, Cork would have won nothing.'

'Nemo are the making of the Cork team.'

'You were the best goalie I ever saw.'

'Pity about the defeat to Fermanagh. You're so right too, there's no talent coming through. It's all the fault of the system.'

What not to say:

'Only for Tompkins and Fahy sure ye'd never have won the All-Ireland.'

'What happened against Kerry in this year's Munster Championship?'

'That Colin Corkery looks fierce unfit.'

Micky Harte

What to say:

'Tyrone wouldn't have won the All-Ireland without you.'

'Spillane doesn't know what he's talking about.'

'Your son Mark will be the new Peter Canavan.'

What not to say:

'Art McRory and Eugene MacKenna were blackguarded.'

'Ye play puke football.'

'Are you the guy that won *You're a Star* with "We've Got the World Tonight"?'

Joe Kernan

What to say:

'Armagh never got the credit they deserved for winning the All-Ireland in 2002.'

'Spillane made a right fool of himself at half-time in that game.'

'That was a mighty speech you gave in the dressing-room that time.'

'Francie Bellew marks tighter than Kylie Minogue's famous hotpants.'

What not to say:

'The two Brians, Canavan and McAlinden, laid the foundations of Armagh's success.'

'Crossmaglen's dominance is bad for the game in Armagh.'

'Is yer full-back line really slower than Pat Spillane's Ma?'

Jack O'Connor

What to say:

'Páidí stayed on too long.'

'If you got the job in 2002, Kerry would be going for the three-in-a-row now.'

What not to say:

'How many All-Irelands did you win as a player?'

'Were you the manager of the Kerry under-21 team that lost to Waterford last year?'

'Are you anything to Sinéad?'

16

Mighty Meath

Few people are more regularly accused of being of dubious parentage than me, but in Meath they also have a story casting doubts on my intelligence. At the annual dinner of a junior club in the county, the story was told of a plane with five passengers: a grandfather from Meath, his grandson, Joe Brolly, Colm O'Rourke and me. The plane was about to crash but there were only four parachutes. A crisis meeting was held to decide who was going to get the four parachutes.

Joe Brolly was first to speak. 'I'm the greatest footballer Ulster has ever seen. Given my service to the province I have to be saved.' He took the first parachute and jumped out of the plane.

Next up was Colm O'Rourke. He said, 'I'm the finest forward Meath has ever produced. I managed Ireland to success in the Compromise Rules in Australia. For all that, I deserve to live.' He took the second parachute and jumped out of the plane.

Then I got up and said, 'I am the greatest footballer of all time. I won eight All-Ireland medals and nine All-Stars. I'm the biggest name in the GAA. I must be allowed to live.' So I took the third parachute and jumped out of the plane.

At this point the Meath man turned to his grandson, and with tears toppling in steady streams down his cheeks, he said, 'Listen Tiny Tim, you take the last parachute. I've had a long life. You've got your whole life ahead of you.'

Tiny Tim said, 'Don't worry Grandpa, there are still two parachutes left. I gave that aul boll*x Spillane my schoolbag and that's what he jumped out the plane with on his back!'

Meath don't take any prisoners on or off the field. On my last visit to Meath I thought it would be politic to downplay my talents as a player. I was quickly told, 'Don't be so modest. You're not that great.' When I moved to presenter of *The Sunday Game*, former Meath captain, Liam Hayes, said I had switched from, 'chief gobshite to chief interrogator'.

Tuff Stuff

People often say Meath footballers are dogged, determined and stubborn – and that's only the nice things they say about them. A lot of players have the attitude of never going for a 50–50 ball unless they're 80–20 sure of winning it. Meath players never had that problem. In 1996, after the All-Ireland semifinal, two irate Tyrone fans were loud in their condemnation of the Meath team, particularly of the alleged ill-treatment of Peter Canavan. A Meath fan made an interesting and revealing slip of the tongue in response: 'You can't make an omelette without breaking legs.'

Colm O'Rourke and I were analysing that match that night for *The Sunday Game*. One of the most controversial incidents in the game came when Martin O'Connell appeared to stamp on a Tyrone player. There were a lot of calls into the programme about the incident, and the producer decided that Colm and I should discuss it. The problem was that we were watching the incident on a small monitor and were a little bit further away than usual. As a result, I wasn't fully sure what had happened, so I was very wishy washy and gave the benefit of the doubt to O'Connell. Being wishy washy is not something I make a habit of. Colm was not very critical of his former team-mate. Afterwards most people said that's all they would expect from O'Rourke when it came to Meath, but that I had chickened out. I would agree with them! It is probably one of the few times I chickened out as an analyst. When you get into the question of intent, though, it is very hard to prove.

Fast forward to the Leinster semifinal this year, when Meath's John Cullinane stamped on a Laois player. In the analysis afterwards, O'Rourke, without any prompting, immediately said that the unsavoury episode was a 'disgrace to the Meath jersey'. Everyone would agree that Colm is a top-class analyst, but he went up further still in many people's eyes with that refreshingly honest comment.

The late John B. Keane always made the point that the most dangerous animal on the planet was a 40-year-old junior footballer with varicose veins. Watching Meath football down the years, I have often thought about John B. I would say that there have been many stories like that told about various Meath players.

If I was starting my career again I wouldn't fancy making my debut on the likes of Mick Lyons. The lion and the lamb shall lie down together, but the lamb won't get much sleep.

Nice Guys Don't Always Finish Last

I have no problem in saying that Seán Boylan is the second greatest manager I have ever came across in Gaelic football, behind Mick O'Dwyer. He has had a remarkable career at the top level over 22 years. He is an absolute gentleman.

Where Boylan differs from O'Dwyer is that he brought three different teams to All-Ireland glory: the '87 and '88 team, the '96 team and the '99 team. Certainly the team he won the '99 title with featured some very average players. His greatest achievement was that he was able to take very ordinary club players and transform them into ferocious competitors who were willing to die for the Meath jersey.

The jury will always remain out about who was responsible for Meath's at times 'overly robust' tactics. Was it Boylan or was it his senior players? It is something that I have never been able to get an answer to.

I feel sorry for the way it has gone for Boylan in the last two years. I believe he has stayed on too long. He should have stepped down after the defeat to Fermanagh in 2003. He was reappointed again this September, beating Eamon Barry for the third year in a row. Meath followers have a reputation for being very brave, but it is amazing that none of the ex-players had the guts to challenge Boylan, even though they are very critical of him off the record. I am all for loyalty, but sometimes loyalty comes second to what is right for your county. Meath football needs fresh blood at the helm. My worry for Seán is that he could easily be caught in the same situation as Páidí Ó Sé was in Kerry, and be humiliated and pushed out before he can jump. I think he should go now.

Spin City

At the start of the Championship this year, I put Meath as number one on my list of 'no-hopers'. I wrote:

> *Seán Boylan's attempt to build a third All-Ireland winning side smacks a little of a manager who might have stayed on just that bit too long. His elder servants that remain are beginning to suggest that they have given their best days, while the youngsters have only shown glimpses of what is needed to compete at the top level in inter-county level.*

Laois's comprehensive victory over Meath in the Leinster semifinal suggests that, for once, I was right. Nonetheless I have to take my hat off yet again to Boylan. He came on television straight after the defeat and said that Laois won because they were the better team. As always, he was gracious and magnanimous in defeat.

What always impresses me about Boylan in those situations is that he doesn't attempt to spin. Sadly, spinning is something that managers are very fond of doing today. This again shows a tendency to ape everything in other sports. Early this year, Ireland lost its opening Six Nations rugby match to France. Irish coach Eddie O'Sullivan spun the result very well. He said Ireland took a lot of positives out of it. The statistics showed that:

- Ireland won 22 lineouts, France only won 7.
- Ireland won six mauls, France only won one.
- Ireland won 56 rucks, France only 50.
- Ireland won 33 balls in the opposition's 22, France only won 10.
- Ireland spent 49 minutes and 2 seconds in the opposition's half, France only spent 35 minutes and 52 seconds in our half.
- Ireland only made 16 errors, France made 19.

With those impressive statistics Ireland must have won comfortably. No. Ireland lost by 18 points. Eddie's spinning still wasn't finished, though. He pointed out that we finished strongly and we never gave up. Subsequent events proved Eddie O'Sullivan was right to be optimistic, because Ireland won the Triple Crown in 2004. The main reason why I was annoyed about his comments after the France game was that it reminded me that we are a great nation for moral victories. It is something that I'm always harping on about, because I think our eagerness to celebrate moral victories is detrimental to the possibility of us achieving the ultimate success. Ireland took a huge moral victory out of winning the Triple Crown this year, but to me the key fact was that we only finished second in the Championship.

What was even worse was the way we celebrated limping out of the soccer World Cup in both 1994 and 2002. Who will ever forget when Albert Reynolds was photographed with big Jack when the team returned from USA '94? It was like Charlie Haughey and Stephen Roche in 1987 all over again. Then off for a damp squib of a concert shown live on national television in the Phoenix Park. Then, in 2002, it was back to the Phoenix Park again for another celebration live on RTÉ, and for Joe Duffy to ask Damien Duff about his Padre Pio medal. On both occasions we were being asked to celebrate defeats to Holland and Spain respectively.

Forgive me if I'm cynical, but I come from a county where success is delivering a trophy at the end of the day and anything less than winning is failure. It sums up the psyche of Kerry footballers to say that second best is not tolerated. When you do tolerate second best, accepting failure is much easier. Seán Boylan is someone who is never happy to be second best.

Happy Days Are Not Here Again

Meath people are pining for another chance to regain the All-Ireland title. How realistic is that in the short term? A story serves to illustrate.

One day Seán Boylan was walking by the Hill of Tara with his poodle. He was walking slowly as his poodle has only three legs when he came across a bottle. When he unscrewed the top of the bottle, a genie appeared and said, 'I'm so grateful to get out of that bottle that I will grant you one wish.'

Seán thought for a moment and said, 'I have always dreamed that my poodle would win the major prize at Crufts, but that's not possible as he only has three legs. Could you give him a fourth leg please.'

The genie thought for a moment and then said, 'I'm sorry, I can't do that. Just think of all the operations that would be involved in putting the leg together. I'm sorry, but could you ask for an easier wish?'

Boylan said, 'Well there is one other thing. I'd like to train Meath to win one more All-Ireland.'

The genie thought about it for a few minutes and then said, 'So what kind of paws do you want on that new leg for your poodle?'

17

The Top 10 GAA Boo-Boos

The year 2004 has seen the GAA at various levels shooting itself in the foot yet again in a wide variety of ways. Here is my list of Top 10 GAA blunders this year. I had initially thought of recording the all-time top GAA blunders, but that list was way too long.

1. Ex-Presidents of the GAA finding fault with the motion to discuss Rule 42.

Their attempt to hide from the shifting sands of time is the GAA equivalent of turkeys voting for Christmas.

2. The decision that a hurling match in the mid-Tipperary club Championship had effectively precedence over a Tipperary–Fermanagh qualifier.

This led to Tipperary's decision to withdraw from the football Championship. What sort of statement must this make to Declan Browne, one of the greatest artists in the game today?

3. Having the draw for the hurling Qualifiers before Offaly played Wexford.

4. The designation of the 'weaker counties'.

There were some very strange choices in this category. Longford were designated a weaker county, which is a surprise considering that they had played in Division One this year and topped it for a period. At least common sense prevailed when they agreed to play

Waterford, whose Championship record in the last 20 years has been dismal, at a neutral venue.

Likewise Derry got home advantage against Cavan. It is bizarre that Derry are considered a designated county, considering they had got to the All-Ireland semifinal just three years ago, and actually won the All-Ireland eight years previously.

5. GAA travel arrangements.

London travelled to play Dublin in the Qualifiers the morning of the match on a 7.45 am flight. How could anyone be expected to give their best in those circumstances? Some of the big gamblers in the GAA, who bet tens of thousands of euro using the handicap system, when they got on the Internet and discovered the travelling arrangements, really hit the bookies hard. If you think it about it, when 15 guys leave their homes in some parts of London at 5 am to catch an early morning fight and then have to play against a Dublin team that is fully fit and hurting from losing to Westmeath, there can only be one outcome.

6. Umpiring mistakes all year.

Brian Morley gets a point for Westmeath when it should be a wide. Offaly lose the match by a point and go out of the Leinster Championship. Westmeath go on to win the Leinster title.

7. Rory O'Connell's suspension.

As the court subsequently proved, proper procedures were not followed in this case. Rory was sent off for allegedly 'striking' an opponent. Yet the Offaly player involved, Pascal Kellaghan, wrote in to say he had not in fact been struck in the way Rory was accused of. Yet the GAA didn't see fit to consider Kellaghan's testimony. Natural justice was denied. Many would say not for the first time in the GAA.

Rory can play on until the GAA appeal his case, but the GAA won't appeal because it will cost them money and they will probably lose anyway. I think the courts will increasingly become part of the furniture of Gaelic games. Any county or club that has a wealthy benefactor that has a player suspended is going to appeal it in the courts. They have every chance because the GAA has neither the money nor the stomach for a protracted and expensive legal struggle. The countless number of tireless volunteers around the country who keep the GAA going will not want to see the fruits of their labour going into the pockets of fat cat lawyers.

An interesting situation arose this year that I believe will store up a lot of trouble in this context for the GAA in the future. Cork and Tipperary have a home and away arrangement for the Munster Championship, but when they were drawn against each other in the Qualifiers, Tipperary argued that the Qualifiers was a separate competition and that the home and away system did not apply in this situation. To my mind, the GAA created a significant precedent when they ruled that the Qualifiers was a separate competition. I think this will have legal implications down the road. Take the case of Waterford's John Mullane, who was sent off in the Munster Championship and subsequently suspended for the All-Ireland semifinal. Could he not have gone to court and argued that the All-Ireland semifinal was a separate competition and he should be allowed to play in it? In fairness to Waterford they did not go down that route, but I certainly can see other counties doing so in the future.

8. The Tommy Murphy Cup.

This seemed like a good idea at the time. The weaker counties are always complaining that they do not get enough games – even though they get at least two now. What happens when they establish a competition to give them more games? Only five teams entered. One of them, London, pulled out almost straight away. Sligo entered but their then county manager, James

Kearins, refused to train the team because he said the competition was no use. Star players were not interested either. The Sligo County Board had to run around, and try to get an interim manager who would train the side only for this competition. What are the weaker counties up to? It seems as if they want their bread buttered on both sides. Can the GAA not sell its own competition to the various County Boards? If they can't sell it to their own people, how can they expect to sell it to a national audience?

9. The directive on managers not criticising referees.

This followed a spate of criticisms, on and off the field, from managers, most notably Brian Cody's incursion on to the pitch against Galway. If managers are suspended for criticising referees, it is inevitable that their cases will end up in the courts. Any barrister worth his salt will bore holes in the GAA's position, because one of the inalienable rights every citizen has under the Irish constitution is the right to free speech. In that context there may be trouble ahead with managers of so-called 'weaker counties'. Earlier this year, Luke Dempsey was quite vocal in his criticism of referees after Carlow were beaten by Laois, and Hugh Kenny, in particular, after Wicklow were beaten by Meath, was quite emotional in claiming that referees discriminate against the weaker counties. I think there is something in that because it is interesting to note that referees appear to interpret directives more leniently in the later rounds of the Championship when only the 'big guns' are still around.

10. The chaos and confusion after the Kilkenny–Clare All-Ireland hurling quarter-final.

After the match is drawn, the teams are exchanging jerseys and the crowd is leaving Croke Park when an announcement is made over the public address system that extra time will be played. Mass head-scratching takes place. There will be extra time. No there won't. Nobody knows what is happening. Players, team management, match commentators, fans, the national television audience are completely in the dark. GAA officials are spotted running around like headless chickens. Eventually another announcement is made that a replay will take place. The fiasco is captured live on television. What's the problem? The *clár an lae* says there will be extra time. How can this embarrassing organisational shambles be tolerated in 2004? It provided yet more ammunition for critics of the GAA to take an easy pot shot.

18

What's Another Year?

I started the 2004 Championship as an ABU – Anybody But Ulster. I feared that Ulster teams were going to be responsible for a brand of Gaelic football that seemed hell-bent into evolving into a joust between powerful packs of barrel-chested men in Lycra. I feared a predominantly defence-oriented game where safety-first tactics were prioritised. This means pulling 13 of your 15 players back behind the half-way line once possession is lost; reducing the margin of error in defence by keeping possession and going forward in a series of solo runs and short, passing movements; and chasing and hunting in packs is now a must for all players, which means an ever-increasing demand on their fitness and stamina levels. Watching Greece winning Euro 2004, I wondered if they were secretly coached by either Joe Kernan or Mickey Harte. As Eamon Dunphy said recently, if you want to find entertainment, go the cinema because you won't find it in sport. In 2002 and 2003, playing positive attacking football was about as useful as trying to empty Kenmare Bay with a fork. The sad reality is that these cancers have spread throughout the country. Most tragically of all, even my beloved Kerry had succumbed to this disease, a fact that was graphically illustrated in the Munster final, in particular during the drawn match. After the drawn match, a change could be seen in Kerry's tactics, there were elements of defensive play, but the main emphasis was once again on positive football.

It has got to the stage now, though, that we are going to have to change the language of positional play. Most teams today no longer have half-forwards whose main job it is to score. Instead their main job is to play in front of the half-back line and stop the other team from scoring. Where is the evidence for this, I hear you ask. In the 1986 All-Ireland final I scored 1–4 from play. At the time there was nothing unusual in that. I was there to score. This year in four games in the Munster Championship, the entire Kerry half-forward line scored 1–7 between them. In last year's All-Ireland final, the Tyrone half-forward line scored two points between the three of them. We should now be calling half-forwards something like 'the extra back-line' or 'the third line of defenders'.

I am still not convinced by all these new methods teams are going in for today. To take one example, it is now accepted orthodoxy in the GAA world that the night before big games, teams use a 'buddy system' in the hotel. In other words, a senior player rooms with one of the more junior players on the panel. The idea is that the senior player helps the younger man to settle and handle his nerves better. I do not go along with that at all. I think you should room with the player you want to room with, rather than finding yourself rooming with someone you have nothing in common with. In 1991, on the night before the All-Ireland semifinal I found myself rooming with a young sub on the Kerry team. I always liked to relax the night before a match by staying up late and watching television. My roommate, though, wanted to go to bed early, and I felt obliged to do so the same for his sake. The problem was that because I was deviating from my normal routine, I could not sleep at all, and therefore it was very hard to be at my best playing a huge match the next day. Well that's my feeble excuse anyway!

Until the quarter-finals, the Championship did not really lift off this year. Some of the teams I had looked to to inject a bit of panache into the proceedings, like Dublin, were a disappointment. The reason for their shortcomings is most tellingly revealed in a story I heard recently: The good news is that Saddam Hussein is going to get the death penalty. The bad news is it's going to be taken by one of the Dublin forwards.

After losing to Westmeath in the Leinster Championship, the Dublin fans had to leave Croke Park behind for less salubrious venues like Carrick-on-Shannon. The hard-pressed Leitrim County Board had a nasty surprise though, when the Dublin fans took all their balls. We have had the 'Free the Birmingham Six' campaign and the 'Free the Guildford Four' campaign. I want to launch the 'Free the Leitrim balls' campaign.

There were all too few flashes of brilliance in the Championship. Westmeath's historic breakthrough was an obvious exception. Also in that category came Mattie Forde's tour de force in scoring 2–10 (with only two points from frees) in Wexford's 2–14 to 0–15 defeat of Offaly in the Qualifiers. Forde has put his name in lights this year, notably when scoring 4–5 against Galway in the League, and scoring eight goals and 36 points in total during the League.

Ten years ago Danoli became known as the 'People's Champion'. This year the 'People's Team' has been Fermanagh. Their performance against Cork was a particular highlight. Here were 15 guys who were written off but who believed they could do it, and in the process played nice, positive football. Some of the plaudits must go to their manager Charlie Mulgrew. He took the job when nobody else wanted it and got them to play with some style. They appeared to have been unlucky to draw Armagh, the favourites for the All-Ireland, in the quarter-finals, but they pulled off the shock of the season to win and really put it up to Mayo in the semifinal and the replay.

The Homes of Donegal

The first great managerial feat this year came when Donegal beat Tyrone in the Ulster semifinal. The Donegal manager Brian McEniff beat Tyrone at their own game and in that respect he gave a clue to every other manager as to what it takes to beat Tyrone. It is very, very simple. Once Tyrone's half-forwards lose possession, they run back and stand in front of the opposing full-forward line and normally the half-backs of the opposing team are sucked up the field to follow the Tyrone half-forwards, which makes the blanket even more congested. What McEniff did that day was to keep the Donegal half-back line in their original positions, so when Tyrone counter-attacked to try to get the ball into their three main forwards, they were blocked by the Donegal half-back line, who had remained in their places. It is just one more example of McEniff's very keen footballing brain.

It was downhill all the way after that. It all came unstuck for Donegal against Armagh and later Fermanagh in the Qualifiers. If I was in McEniff's shoes, what would alarm me the most was the lack of discipline that was apparent in the Fermanagh game when Donegal player Brendan Devenney was sent off in normal time, after needlessly tripping his man. Then Stephen McDermott was sent off in extra-time for an equally pointless foul.

However, McEniff would rank up there as being as cute as Mick O'Dwyer, and that would be as high a compliment as you could give. He's the same sort of guy as O'Dwyer in the sense that when you are talking to him, you think you are asking him questions, but he's really picking your brain. He was a very intelligent and stylish footballer himself, and one of the best defenders in the game in the early 1970s. In 2003 he was the County Chairman and the Central Council delegate, as well as team manager. He did everything but drive the bus and wash the jerseys. As a manager he really shone after Donegal's defeat to Fermanagh in 2003. In that match they gave an abysmal performance, but McEniff picked them off the floor to bring them within a whisker of qualifying for an All-Ireland final which was an absolutely incredible achievement.

I was opposed to his appointment as manager of the Irish International Rules team, however. The first year he was in charge the team were beaten. In fairness by the second year he had the team much better prepared for their trip to Australia.

The Harte of the Matter

Those who said Tyrone were finished after the defeat to Donegal received a rude awakening in the Qualifiers. It was a telling sign of the times that before Tyrone played Galway, Tyrone manager Mickey Harte explained in the most-matter-of-fact voice that his son, Mark, would miss the match because he had pulled a muscle aquajogging. It's a big change from Paddy Bawn Brosnan's time.

Harte is serious and very astute. His record as a manager at minor and under-21 is unrivalled, and the final part of his CV came last year when he delivered Sam to Tyrone. With that kind of track record it is very hard to find flaws in his game. He is a very serious thinker about the tactical side of the game and certainly outmanoeuvred Paidí Ó Sé in last year's semifinal. He is a stickler for statistics. This year his biggest challenge was to get his Tyrone team to rekindle the appetite, work-rate, commitment and hunger that so epitomised their success last year. Against Mayo they just could not reclaim that intensity, and they lost the quarter-final to a hungrier team.

Of course, what made Tyrone's 2002 All-Ireland victory all the sweeter was that it came over their old rivals, Armagh. A story goes that four men went climbing a mountain, each claiming to be the most loyal fan in the country: one was from Armagh, one from Tyrone, one from Tipperary and one from Waterford. When they climbed the mountain the Tipp fan said, 'This is how much

I love Tipperary.' With that he jumped off the mountain and died instantly.

The Waterford fan said, 'This is how much I love Waterford.' With that he jumped off the mountain and died instantly.

The Tyrone man said, 'This is how much I love Tyrone.'

With that he pushed the Armagh man off the mountain.

Blind Analyst's Bluff

When you work in the print media, one of the occupational hazards for a journalist is that you have to write pen-pictures before games. I hate writing pen-pictures of the Tyrone half-back line because I find it incredibly hard to identify them as to me they all look the same and they all have the same style of play, they are all like terriers. If one of them stood right in front of me I wouldn't know which of them it was. This makes it very hard to get variety into your pen-pictures and, the odd time, out of sheer desperation, you have to bluff. This ploy brings its own hazards.

Before the 1995 All-Ireland, I was asked to write pen-pictures of some of the Tyrone back-line. When it came to one of their midfielders, Jody Gormley, I couldn't for the life of me get a mental picture of him in my head, so I wrote what I thought were banal comments about him. One of them was that he 'lacks a bit of pace'. The day after the match I met Jody in the reception at the Burlington Hotel and he said, 'I was very hurt by what you wrote. I'm the fastest member of the Tyrone team!'

I had to admit to him that I was only bluffing. This is one of the golden rules for an analyst: If you can't convince, confuse!

Since my 'puke football' comments last year, there have been many comments about me made by the Tyrone people, including:

- 'It's time for Spillane to gather up his belongings and get off the TV. All footballers are sick listening to him and he is no good for the game.'

- 'Spillane is nothing but a waste of time, running parallel to his own column.'
- 'What Spillane does is make sure he's talked about all week but it's not exactly a novel tactic, after all Eamon Dunphy has been doing it for years.'
- 'Spillane's comment about puke football should be interpreted as <u>P</u>ure <u>U</u>nadulterated <u>K</u>erry <u>E</u>mbarrassment.'
- 'Spillane has lost all credibility as a TV pundit. Someone from Ulster must've done something bad to him in the previous life. He is so anti-Ulster all the time.'
- The *pièce de resistance,* though, has got to be: 'Pat Spillane, what can you expect from a sickening dose but "puke"?'

The Boys from the County Armagh

In April, before the Championship started I listed Armagh as number three behind Meath and Derry on my list of 'no-hopers':

> *This ageing team badly needed a good League campaign to unearth some new talent. None emerged. Now Armagh face into the 2004 Championship with the same faces and formula that has seen them be very competitive in the All-Ireland every year since 1999. That's a long time on the go with the same bunch. They may be going to the well once too often this summer.*

What happens? They have a real rollercoaster of a Championship. They looked great against Monaghan, though Monaghan put up feeble resistance. Then they struggled to beat 14-man Cavan. That was a game when the unthinkable happened: I lavished great praise on the match referee, Michael Monahan! He had the courage to break an unwritten rule and sent off a Cavan player in the very first minute. Armagh played glorious football against Donegal in Croke Park and were immediately installed as hot favourites for the All-Ireland, though Fermanagh really shocked them in the quarter-final.

Much of the credit for Armagh's success in the last three years must go to Joe Kernan. Joe is a larger-than-life individual and a great raconteur. He is a bit like Páidí Ó Sé in many ways, including the fact that they both possess a much underestimated footballing brain. As Joe is such a gregarious character, there is a danger of people missing his inner strength and brilliance. He has a superb record at club level with Crossmaglen and was the final piece in the jigsaw that was needed to bring an All-Ireland to Armagh. To me it seemed he had inherited an Armagh team close to the end of the line. But, he reinvigorated them and got what looked like a tired team at the end of its road back on the track to ultimate glory. I like the way they seemed to play with a lot more joy this year. They put in an awesome performance in the Ulster final while on the same day the so-called aristocrats, Kerry, were completely uninspiring in the Munster final. Maybe I've got it wrong about Ulster football all these years!

Kernan, in common with a lot of other great managers in recent years – like Liam Griffin, Seán Boylan, Brian McEniff, Páidí Ó Sé and Mick O'Dwyer – is a very successful businessman and I think that is significant. One thing I like about Joe is that he is one of the managers like Anthony Daly, Mickey Harte, John O'Mahony, Micko, Páidí and Seán Boylan who are not running along the sidelines with ear-pieces in their ears. I am always intrigued when I see managers with ear-pieces. Who are they talking to? It is all part of a fad and it highlights a problem we have in Gaelic football today – style over substance. Wearing an ear-piece is a sign that you have an extra edge. I always think part of the ruination of Gaelic football came when the PE teacher came on the scene as coach and manager. At the time there was a few bob floating around for coaching, and they had to be seen to bring something extra to the mix to earn their fee. As a result, they brought in cones and introduced drills, which was the first step in complicating the game. Again I go back to Micko's training with us. For the first half hour the forwards just kicked balls into the goal and the backs caught them and kicked them back out to us. The key skills were there in that exercise.

No Afternoon Tea Party

What did not surprise me about the Ulster final was that there was nothing for the players in Croke Park, not even a cup of tea after the game. I have been down this road myself many times during my playing days. I can recall going to play in games to open so-called 'state of the art' stadia like Páirc Uí Chaoimh, only to discover that the dressing-rooms would at best be suitable for a team of pygmies or to discover that there was no toilet roll in the players' toilets. I can still remember trying to get a drink with Ger Lynch and my brother Tom in Croke Park after winning the All-Ireland in 1984 only to be told, 'Sorry, VIPs only.' DJ Carey has a similar story about trying to use one of the lifts in Croke Park only to be refused with the words, 'This is a lift for VIPs only.'

In the GAA there is a very definite hierarchy when it comes to big games. At the top of the list are the VIPs. Then just underneath them come the corporate people and sponsors. Then comes the officials of all sorts. Supporters come a distant fourth and players come fifth. The gap has narrowed a little since my day, but only a little.

The Derry Air

Derry were number two on my list of no-hopers before the Championship. After a dire start against Tyrone, they moved up a few gears and reached the All-Ireland semifinals. As you can imagine, slagging me off is the number-one pastime in Derry!

At a fund-raising function for the Derry team, one of the organisers told an old story about me in which I appeared with Gay Byrne on the TV show *Who Wants to be a Millionaire?* I had reached the €16,000 mark, and if I got the next question right, I would have won a small fortune, but if I got it wrong I lost practically everything. Gaybo said, 'Ah yes, I think you will have no problem with this question. On screen is a photograph of an Irish sporting legend from Cork as a small baby. Who is it?'

'Okay,' I replied, looking nervous, 'I'm sure it's Sonia O'Sullivan, that's my final answer.'

There was a tense drum roll and the music dipped before Gaybo spoke again.

'Sorry, Pat, you were wrong. Thanks for playing.'

As the audience start to clap sympathetically I asked, 'What was the correct answer, it's killing me?'

Gaybo replied, 'Roy Keane!'

Losing the Siege of Limerick

Derry qualified for the All-Ireland quarter-final by defeating Limerick in Hyde Park, Roscommon. This should have been Limerick's year. In the Munster Championship, Clare tried to narrow the pitch against Kerry bringing back defenders, and Kerry really struggled against them. Limerick tried to do the same against Kerry. Seemingly the hitting, on and off the ball, was ferocious. Unfortunately for Limerick, Kerry decided they were no longer going to be the whipping boys and decided to meet fire with fire. It is very hard to turn nice boys into demons. But Kerry players were very naïve, and every time a Kerry fella hit an opponent they were caught on camera. The next day I was at the Killarney races where a number of people told me that I had been very hard on Kerry in my match analysis. I said we could have picked another six or seven incidents showing Kerry players striking their opponents. The Kerry County Chairman told me that a lot of Kerry players were being constantly struck off the ball, in particular it seems that 'Gooch' and Mike Frank were being pulled and hit off the ball in front of the umpires who just stood stupidly there without drawing the referee's attention to these incidents. Umpires need to become more actively involved in assisting the referee to combat off-the-ball stuff. As Billy Keane, son of the much-missed John B., observed, 'The Munster final had more fouls than you would find in a turkey farm the week before Christmas.'

Three times this year, in the League semifinal, the Munster final and the Munster final replay, Limerick had the chance to beat Kerry. Each time they choked. Opportunities like those don't come by too often, and they should have taken at least one of them. The psychological wounds from these defeats will be hard to heal.

Kerry, though, save the best for last. They went on and showed their true class in their demolition job of Mayo in the All-Ireland final. Fair play to Jack O'Connor. He delivered Sam to Kerry for the 33rd time in his first year. That is all that matters in the kingdom, because, as ABBA told us, 'The Winner Takes it All!' Good for Jack for sticking to his guns, deploying players with a great work ethic and a harder edge, like Paul Galvin who delivered the goods for him big time.

I have to confess that I did not expect Kerry to do such a demolition job on Mayo in the All-Ireland final. At least I didn't go as far as Páidí Ó Sé and publicly predict Mayo would win Sam! Kerry has done Gaelic football a big favour by putting the ball back in fashion. Other teams please copy. The reason, though, why Kerry won their 33rd title is that a win like that is quickly forgotten in the Kingdom. A day or two after winning a final, Kerry people immediately start thinking about winning the next one, and that has been a major part of their success story to date. That's also why Dara Ó Cinnéide did not need to say anything about the critics when he accepted the Sam Maguire trophy.

At 7 o'clock on the evening of the All-Ireland final, I received a text from Tommy Lyons. It simply read: 'Football's going home.' That said it all.

How the West Was Won

Gaelic football is in a state of chaos. I was in the depths of depression watching Kerry in the Munster final but exhilarated watching Mayo in the Connacht final. I even found myself praising the Mayo forward line. Has the world gone mad?

There is a general rule of thumb that I believe carries a fair amount of weight: that teachers, priests, army men and guards do not in the long run make great managers because they are used to getting their own way, are disciplinarians, like the sound of their own voice and are not the greatest of communicators. I am a teacher myself, and I know I would not make it as a manager for those reasons. John Maughan, however, did an excellent job with Clare and Mayo. As an army man, he made his mark as a manager by being a strict disciplinarian and a fitness fanatic. I am not meaning to criticise those two qualities, but the problem with getting teams so fit and disciplined is that they can only get you so far. They will get you over many fences but not the final ones. It is interesting that Maughan's team failed at the second last hurdle with Clare and three times now at the last hurdle in the case of Mayo. It is a matter of fact that he brought no success to Fermanagh. He was tactically naïve in the way he left Pat Holmes on Maurice Fitzgerald for the 70 minutes in the 1997 All-Ireland final. Anybody could have seen Holmes was getting an almighty roasting. The situation where Dermot Flanagan was passed fit to play in an All-Ireland when everyone knew he was injured was another bad call. The proof was in the pudding when he had to be taken off after only a few minutes and it took about six switches to cover his position, which caused a lot of disruption in the Mayo defence. I believe, though, that Maughan's management skills and tactical ability have come on mightily in recent years.

We got a lot of criticism into *The Sunday Game* after Joe Brolly and Colm O'Rourke's repeated comments about the Mortimer brothers and Kieran McDonald's hairstyle during the Connacht final. Around this time there was also a lot of media speculation that Sven-Göran Eriksson would lose his job as English coach because of his sexual indiscretions in the 'Fariagate' scandal. My attitude to all of this is very simple. If you are the Kerry manager, I don't care if you are homosexual, heterosexual or metrosexual as long as you lead Kerry to the All-Ireland. If you are a Kerry forward I don't care how you score in your private life as long as you score frequently on the pitch, and I don't care if you wear hair-bands, lipstick or frilly knickers as long as you can steer the ball between the posts.

Mayo played some nice football to reach the All-Ireland this year, but even in their triumphs I annoyed Mayo people yet again by saying that their opponents, New York, Galway and Roscommon, were not up to much. A correspondent from Mayo took great pleasure in emailing *The Sunday Game* to announce that the most recent comment doing the rounds about me in Mayo is, 'Pat Spillane can't bear fools. Pity his mother didn't have the same problem.'

Hard Men and Girl Power

One of the features of the media coverage of the GAA this year has been the number of articles about the increased incidence of violence. The case for the prosecution can be summed up as follows:

- The Henry Shefflin incident.
- The fracas after the Cork–Laois minor quarter-final.
- In Longford, inter-county referee Eugene Murtagh was sent off in a junior football match in July for verbally abusing the referee Mick Doherty. Murtagh was playing for his club Seán Connolly's against Mostrim and took umbrage with Doherty's decision to sideline his son, Eugene Jnr.

- In a hurling match between Pallasgreen and Bruree in July, a mass brawl broke out, and after a five-minute battle, the referee abandoned the game.

- After the Munster football final referee Gerry Kinneavy had to be escorted from the pitch by the Gardaí.

- Even in Kerry there has been aggro. Gerard Lynch was refereeing a club match in Tralee when he received a blow to the jaw as he was sending off a player.

- Surprise, surprise there was an 'incident' in Wicklow. St Patrick's club banned two members for life after a violent incident at a hurling match arising from an internal dispute when officials were abused and a female supporter was struck on the head with a hurl.

- Just to show that we have now entered an equal opportunities era, women in Wicklow have been getting in one the act. At a camogie match between Kiltegan and Annacurra there was a full-scale pitch battle with players, mentors and some supporters flexing their muscles.

In fact I actually think violent incidents are more isolated now than they were in the past. The big difference now is that there is so much media exposure, whether local or national, that nothing is missed and many incidents are magnified. Of course we cannot condone them, but they are symptomatic of what is happening in society, particularly among the young where there is a creeping aggressiveness surfacing and they are much more likely to engage in confrontation.

Often in these situations it is impossible to adjudicate on intent. I have learned this from personal experience. During the infamous Meath–Tyrone All-Ireland semifinal in 1996 there were two incidents when I found myself in that very rare position for me of not knowing what to say. John McDermott knocked over Peter Canavan. The more you looked at it, the more you could find a reason to argue vehemently that he did it deliberately, but equally you could claim with the same conviction that it was an accident. An even more controversial incident occurred when Martin O'Connell was alleged to have stamped on Brian Dooher when he was on the ground. I could not be sure of O'Connell's intent so I gave him the benefit of the doubt.

I believe that *The Sunday Game* was right to address these issues and I do not believe it was trial by media. We would have abdicated our responsibilities to the viewer had we not tackled these stories head on.

I did, however, have a problem with the reaction to the Cork County Board to our coverage during the summer of the *mêlée* that erupted after the Cork–Laois minor football quarter-final. A Cork mentor had been clearly caught on camera striking a Laois mentor who did not retaliate. Yet far from apologising for the incident, the powers that be in Cork were quick off the blocks to lambaste us for not showing the whole incident. We showed all we had. This was a classic case of shooting the messenger. The scene spoke for itself. The cameras do not lie. The Cork County Board would have been better employed investigating the conduct of their mentors and players rather than attacking RTÉ.

The Anatomy of Success

Every county craves success. Is there a quick fix? No. Limerick used a sport psychologist this year in an effort to make the breakthrough in Munster, but the end result was still the same. One does not have to be a guru to identify what was wrong with Limerick as, believe me, it is not a mental problem. Rather they lack quality forwards. In the Qualifiers against Derry, their forward line scored the grand total of two points. Here's a free piece of advice from somebody who used to know. There is only one way to teach a forward to kick the ball over the bar. It is called practise.

A number of Donegal players had words of inspiration inscribed on their kit for the game against Tyrone. However, those same words of inspiration could not stop them producing two woeful performances against Armagh and Fermanagh.

There is no magic formula for achieving success. If there was the Yanks would probably have discovered it. I believe we adopt too much Americana into Gaelic games. I think of the story of the rowing race between the Japanese and the Americans when the Japanese won by a mile. The Americans spent millions and millions of dollars on consultants to advise them how to reverse the situation. They discovered that the Japanese had eight rowing and one steering whereas the Americans had only one rowing and eight steering. The consultants suggested a corrective plan to put a new structure in place. Their idea was four steering managers, three area-steering managers and a new performance bonus system for the person rowing the boat to provide an incentive. The next year the Japanese won by two miles. The humiliated Americans sacked their rower and gave the bonus to the managers for their excellent recommendation.

I cannot understand why America became the most powerful nation in the world because the Americans I meet are the most gullible people I have ever encountered. Yet we still copy them in sports and take on their ideas on psychologists and gurus, but this merely serves to over-complicate and over-analyse Gaelic football. Above all, it causes teams to concentrate way too much on the opposition, which is unhealthy as worrying about the opposition creates a sense of insecurity. This year this trend even infiltrated hurling. Both Wexford and Clare used tactics to cope with Kilkenny. Clare used a policy of curtailment and confinement to restrict Kilkenny from playing, while Wexford used a policy of exploiting the spaces and taking the Kilkenny players wide.

I would like to dispel two myths about success in sport and business. I think sport and business are practically identical in this respect, because the formula for success is the same. The first myth is: No pain, no gain. All this has done is driven many a person into an early grave. The second myth is: The cream always rises to the top. Euro 2004 proved that this is not true. France, the team with all the stars, limped out of the tournament tamely, whereas Greece, with no stars, won the tournament. I believe the central components of success are commitment and belief, but even these are no good in football if you can't kick a ball.

For my own part, my success as a player was due to a combination of factors: inner drive, belief, hard work and commitment. I was not blessed with natural talent, but I was a slogger and I made sacrifices, worked hard and I was selfish. I was also focused and single-minded. You have to be to make it to the top, as Tiger Woods shows. I was very keen to improve myself. We take many skills that we have for granted without realising that they can be developed further. I was motivated. Motivation is both intrinsic and extrinsic. The best motivation is internal as Labi Siffre wonderfully conveys in the song, 'Something Inside So Strong'. I always had a positive attitude. One technique I used to help me in that respect was visualisation. Before every big game, as we travelled on the bus, I closed my eyes for 20 minutes and visualised every situation that might arise on the pitch. I always saw myself as first to the ball, turning, shooting and scoring. I never once put the ball wide in my visualisation exercise and that helped me to go on to the pitch with a winning attitude.

I always think of the great Kerry team as the prototype of the successful team. We had the four obvious things: we were fit, we trained hard, we were talented and we gave 100 per cent. We had six other ingredients though which made us so successful.

First, we never depended on one or two individuals to produce the goods. If Sheehy and the Bomber were having an off day, the likes of John Egan and Ger Power produced big performances.

Second, we were very much a team. O'Dwyer did not want to see anyone come off the field happy after a defeat. There was no point in saying, 'I played well but the others let me down.' O'Dwyer always drilled into us that we won as a team and we lost as a team.

Third, we were able to handle success – not after 1975 but after the defeats of 1976 and 1977 we were equipped to do so. We used this capacity to motivate us to achieve even more success. We enjoyed it when it came, but we knew it was just a brief interlude until we came back and won again the following year.

Fourth, we had a positive attitude. Each of us always believed that we would beat our man even when we were marking a more skilful player, and collectively, as soon as we put on the Kerry jersey, we believed no team would beat us. That is not arrogance but positive thinking.

Fifth, all the Kerry players were very intelligent. It is vital to a team to have fellas who think about the game, especially about improving their own game, and in particular lads who can read a game, and when things are going badly, never lose their composure and can turn things around.

Finally, we had inspired leadership from Mick O'Dwyer. His man-management skills were excellent, he instilled belief and got us right physically and mentally for the big day. He also knew how to motivate us. When it comes to motivation, it is different strokes for different folks. O'Dwyer knew what buttons to push to motivate us individually and collectively. He always provided us with good feedback. It was always positive feedback, which is more effective than negative. Above all he was a winner. Winners have critical skills, don't leave winning to chance, leave no stone unturned and make things happen.

In the modern game a key to success is the ability to manage stress. Not all stress is bad. If I slept well before an All-Ireland semifinal or final I always played poorly because I was not psyched up. A moderate amount of stress can inspire you to push yourself harder. The problem is when stress leads to burnout, which comes from overload. The example I think of in that context this year was Galway's Michael Meehan. He starred in Caltra's All-Ireland-winning club side and played senior and under-21 football all year for both club and county as well as Sigerson football. It is an indictment of the system that such a talented player is asked to play so much competitive football. It is no wonder that we have so few county footballers still playing in their thirties.

In this context there is also a need to review the Qualifiers when one considers that in four years only three beaten provincial finalists have won their next games. Kevin McStay has drawn attention to the health and safety aspect of top class players playing major games three weekends in a row, as happened to the Laois footballers and the Kilkenny hurlers this year. We treat players as machines but it is vital for them to have rest and recovery time which they don't have at the moment. The players today are like the gladiators in ancient Rome, their welfare is unimportant.

The Dream Team

Earlier this year it emerged that JP McManus had made a gift of 5 million euro to the Limerick County Board. With money like that in the game, there are going to be changes in Gaelic football. Already in club football in Dublin, players are been paid to transfer to big clubs. Inevitably that situation will arise more on the inter-county scene in the not too distant future. So if the transfer system were introduced into Gaelic football tomorrow, which players would be most in demand?

I can now let you in on a big secret. I am to be given the opportunity to build a team from scratch. I can now exclusively reveal the content of a letter I received earlier this year and a preview of my plans to become a county manager next year. My goal is to win an All-Ireland by 2006.

Chelsea FC
Stamford Bridge
London
1 April 2004

Mr Pat Spillane
Templenoeiski
Kerriski
Ireland

> **TOP SECRET. FOR YOUR EYES ONLY.**

Dear Comrade Spillane,

You may have heard of me. I am now in my second year as Chelsea owner, but sadly I have grown disillusioned with soccer. Thanks to your lovely Irish boy, Damien Duff, I have fallen in love with Gaelic football, and I have responded in the only way I know how, by buying out a county team and their stadium. I know the Leitrim county team are at the bottom of the pile at the moment, but I am going to change all that. I am keeping it a secret until Christmas when I move to my new home in Drumshabo and a number of my plans to make Leitrim football sexy will be unveiled. For example, the ground in Carrick-on-Shannon is to become a stadium that will leave Croke Park looking like a ground for a Junior B team in Wicklow. I have also commissioned the Corrs to record a new version of 'Lovely Leitrim'.

I want you to be the new Leitrim manager in 2005. I know you have no experience of mananagement, but I am prepared to give you a chance given your track record as a player. I have to confess that I have spoken to some existing county managers, but even with all my roubles I couldn't afford the money they were looking for. I had no idea that a GAA manager would cost me more than José Mourinho.

If you take the Leitrim job, I will offer you exactly the same salary as José. I hope, unlike some of your peers in Ireland, that will not require a drop in salary on your part.

I will be putting 100 million euro at your disposal to buy players. I have copies of *The Sunday Game* sent over to me every Monday morning so I know my Mike Frank Russell from my Frank Lampard. I would appreciate it if you could send me the details of the team you would like to buy, with six subs, and how you propose to spend my 100 million euro.

I will arrange for my private jet to fly you over to see a Premiership game with me in my Executive Box to discuss this further. As I am told you like exciting football, you will be my guest when Arsenal visit.

I look forward to meeting you then, and to seeing your vision for the new Leitrim team.

Yours sincerely,
Roman Abramovich (you can call me 'Sir'),

Chief Executive,
Lovely Leitrim.

Pat Spillane
Templenoe
Kerry
Ireland
2 April 2004

Roman Abramovich
Chelsea FC
Stamford Bridge
London

Dear Roman,

Thank you for your kind offer. I've always loved Leitrim and would be be delighted to become their boss in 2005.

Attached is my shopping list for my chosen team and the price I expect to pay for each player.

I look forward to discussing this further when we meet for the Arsenal game.

Up Leitrim!

Yours sincerely,
Pat Spillane

Team Leitrim, 2005-6

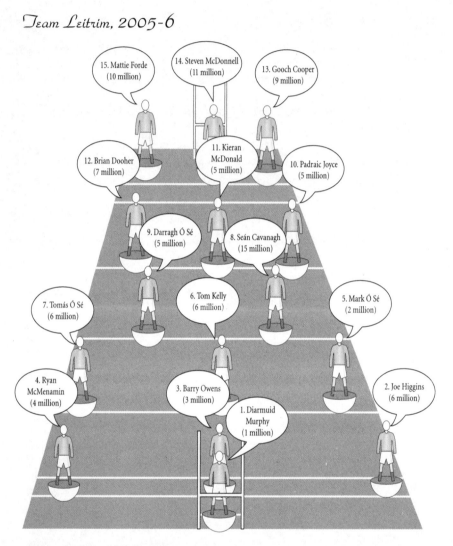

Subs (Budget 5 million)

Gary Connaughton, Graham Canty, Seamus Moynihan, Ciaran MacManus, Dessie Dolan, Declan Browne.

(Note: Mr Abramorich, as some of these subs are coming towards the end of their careers, I will be invoking the Bosman rule, and expect to get them on a free transfer.)

The Sixty Million Dollar Man

Who is the greatest player in Gaelic football today? There are a number of players who might be considered for this accolade. All of the front-runners have many of the attributes that you would be searching for, but equally they would all have limitations. Let us suppose, though, that you could get a top scientist to make a composite of the ideal player. The result would look like something like this:

1. He would have Seamus Moynihan's brain, which secretes intuitive footballing intelligence.

2. The eyes which determine the vision must belong to Peter Canavan.

3. His mouth would come from Kieran McGeeney's because of his ability to inspire and rally his troops and give excellent directions which can turn a game when it is going the wrong way.

4. Sadly the art of fielding and using the hands to catch and release the ball is dying out but there are thankfully masters of the art still surviving so the left arm and hand would be provided by Enda Muldoon ...

5. and the right by Darragh Ó Sé.

6. Given the physical nature of the game, it is vital to have incredible upper body strength so Paul McGrane will provide the chest.

7. With the virtual elimination of the old-style positional play, the game today requires so much running that a good 'engine' is vital. Accordingly, Sean Cavanagh will supply the lungs.

8. You want someone who will never, ever quit. So the heart has to come from Brian Dooher. Like Celine Dion, his heart will go on and on and on.

9. An effective arse is a much neglected weapon in a player's arsenal, because it is great for brushing an opponent aside. For such a bum deal it has to be Diarmuid Marsden.

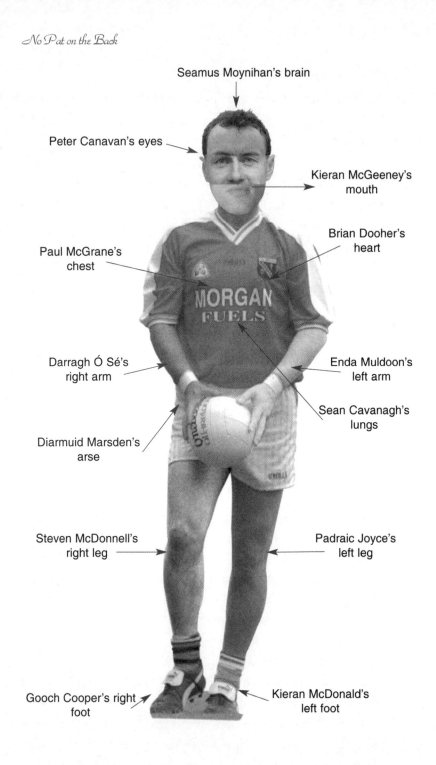

Seamus Moynihan's brain

Peter Canavan's eyes

Kieran McGeeney's mouth

Paul McGrane's chest

Brian Dooher's heart

Darragh Ó Sé's right arm

Enda Muldoon's left arm

Sean Cavanagh's lungs

Diarmuid Marsden's arse

Steven McDonnell's right leg

Padraic Joyce's left leg

Gooch Cooper's right foot

Kieran McDonald's left foot

10. The skill that is most lacking in the game is forwards who can score. Most inter-county forwards today can't kick with one foot let alone two, so our dream player will be equally adept with both feet. If you put together the right leg of Steven McDonnell ...

11. and the right foot of Gooch Cooper ...

12. the left leg of Padraic Joyce ...

13. and the left foot of Kieran McDonald you would have the dream forward.

In fact with all these ingredients you would have the perfect footballer.

The Man in the Mirror

An unexamined life is not worth living. Having critiqued all the teams in this year's Championship, how would I evaluate my own performance as a pundit this year? A recent email from one of my many 'friends' in Tyrone, addressed to me as 'Mr Puke', probably sums up my achievements or lack of them in this regard.

An elderly farmer in a remote part of Carlow finally decided to buy a television. The shopkeeper assured him that this would install the antenna and TV the next day. The next evening the farmer turned on his new TV and found only the same thing on every channel: me presenting *The Sunday Game*. The next morning he turned the TV and found me presenting *The Sunday Game* again no matter what channel he put on. The next day the same thing happened, so he called the shop to complain. The owner said it was impossible for every channel to only have Pat Spillane talking, but agreed to send the repairman to check the TV. When the repairman turned on the TV, he was stunned to find the farmer was right. After looking on the TV for a while he went outside to check the antenna. In a few minutes he returned and told the farmer he had found the problem. The antenna had been installed on top of the windmill and hooked up to the manure spreader.

19

Dear Santa

Dear Santa,

And so it is nearly Christmas and what have you done? It hasn't been a great year in the GAA on or off the field. The standard of football generally left a lot to be desired. Believe me, a lot of my friends in the GAA world need some cheering up this festive season. So here's hoping you can do your best with the list below.

1. For the Ex-Presidents of the GAA – laughing gas. It might at last bring a smile to their glum faces.

2. For Brian Kerr, Eddie O'Sullivan, the FAI and the IRFU – the keys to Croke Park.

3. For Seán Boylan and the Meath football fans – a copy of Perry Como's CD CATCH A FALLING STAR, to remind them that they once had a good team.

4. For Billy Morgan – a Bob the Builder set to help him rebuild his Cork team.

5. For Tommy Lyons and all managers who received P45s this year – a collection of very cuddly toys. They're soft and adorable, just what these fellows need during the dark winter nights in January.

6. For the Leitrim football team – Spider-man suits. It might help them scale a few heights and get them off the bottom rung of the football ladder.

7. For Brian McEniff – a video of Donegal's victory over Tyrone. Please make sure though that he does not get a video of their defeats by Armagh or Fermanagh because they would surely spoil his Christmas dinner.

8. For Mick O'Dwyer – after the year he has had with Laois, I know he would enjoy the board game Frustration.

9. For Joe Brolly – I wanted you to bring him something that would finally help him to drag himself into the Premier League of GAA analysts. I was going to ask for a copy of the HOW TO BE AS GOOD AN ANALYST AS COLM O'ROURKE self-help book but it hasn't been written yet. So just bring him a copy of this book instead!

10. For this humble scribe from Kerry – as I got so many predictions wrong this year, a copy of Murray Walker's book UNLESS I'M VERY MUCH MISTAKEN.

Cheers,

Pat

20

The GAA, Ha, Ha, Ha

Today people are interested in my views about football, not because I was part of the greatest team of all time, though I was! Neither is it because I'm universally recognised as one of the greatest footballers of all time, though I am! My wife assures me I am a legend in my own lunchtime. It is because of my role as a pundit.

As a pundit I have two careers, with the written word in the *Sunday World* and the spoken word on RTÉ. Like Joni Mitchell I have looked at life from both sides now. Kenneth Tynan said: 'A critic is a man who knows the way but can't drive the car.' I was given my jobs in the expectation that I would draw on my own experiences as a player. However, it is the stuff you learn after you know it all that really counts.

I have not always been welcomed with open arms, though. There is certainly a resentment between the traditional journalist and the so-called celebrity analyst. I know that animosity exists, and I've even found the once or twice I've been in the press room in Croke Park where there is tea and coffee that there was a coolness towards me from some journalists for infringing on 'their' territory.

I've only once gone into the press box at a GAA ground. It was at the National League Game between Kerry and Cavan that was played in New York in 1997. It was only for a few minutes and I was simply trying to kill time so I went in for a chat with my

Sunday World colleague, Seán McGoldrick. I was approached by a journalist from a newspaper who abused me strongly for being there when, as he saw it, I had 'no right to be'.

It's Only Words

In 1991 when I joined the *Sunday World*, they were very clear that they didn't want me sitting on the fence. They told me to tell it exactly as I see it, that Cork are going to win because Kerry are useless or Kerry are going to win because Cork are useless (which is usually right).

My local priest expressed concern that I was working with the newspaper in case my morals would be contaminated. He quoted Leo Tolstoy at me: 'All newspaper and journalistic activity is an intellectual brothel from which there is no retreat.'

Things are open to interpretation in the written word. To illustrate this, I think of the story of the little girl who is attacked by a vicious Alsatian in Sneem. She is rescued by a young man who comes along and saves the day by killing the Alsatian. *The Kerryman* newspaper sends a journalist down to cover the story. He tells the locals that it is a great story and says, 'Tomorrow *The Kerryman* newspaper will have a story headlined: "Local football star saves girl".'

The locals patiently explain to him that he can't do that because the young man doesn't play football. The journalist thinks a moment and says, 'That's okay. We'll put: "Kerry man saves girl from Alsatian".'

The locals explain that he can't do that because the young man is a recent blow-in. The following day the headline that appeared in *The Kerryman* was: 'Evil monster kills family pet.'

With the written word, not only can you put an angle on something, you can also wriggle out of things. It is a bit like the story of the panda who meets the prostitute as he is walking down the street and asks her, 'Any chance of a quickie?'

The prostitute brings the panda back to her bedroom and they have sex. After the deed is done, the panda is about to leave when the prostitute says, 'Excuse me, you haven't paid me for this.'

The panda replies, 'What do you mean?'

'I'm a prostitute.'

'I don't understand.'

The prostitute gets a flash of inspiration and says, 'Wait a minute I'll get a dictionary. Here it is. A prostitute: A person who is paid for having sex.'

The panda grabs the dictionary and says: 'Let's look at the definition of a panda. Ah, yes. That's me covered. Look. Panda: Eats, shoots and leaves.'

As well as using the written word to evade trouble, you can also talk your way out of things. It is like the story of the man on his death bed who had five sons, four are giants but tiny Tim was a scrawny little fella. With almost his last breath, John asked Mary, 'Is tiny Tim really mine?'

Mary replied straight from the heart, 'Oh, John he is. I swear to God.'

With that a smile crossed John's face and he died peacefully. Mary whispered a soft prayer, 'Thanks be to you God for not letting him ask about the other four.'

It's true that you can talk your way out of trouble, but if you are anything like me you are more likely to talk your way into trouble! It is like the former Kerry footballer who, although he was married, had 'a roving eye'. The player in question was sitting at home quietly one evening reading his newspaper when his wife sneaked up behind him and whacked him around the head with a frying pan. 'What was that for?' he asked.

'I was doing your washing for you and going through your trousers pocket I found a piece of paper with the name Simone on it and a number after it.'

'Don't be so stupid,' the footballer replied. 'Two weeks ago I backed a horse called Simone and she won. The number was my bookies. You remember when I brought you home that dozen of roses, well I bought them with my winnings. I'm sorry now I bothered.'

'Oh darling, I'm so sorry,' replied his wife. 'How can you ever forgive me?'

The next evening the player was again at home reading his paper. Again his wife sneaked up behind him and whacked him on the head with the frying pan, this time knocking him out cold. When he came around, he asked again: 'What was that for?'

His wife answered through gritted teeth, 'Your f***ing horse phoned.'

Trade Secrets

The biggest influence on my style as a pundit was Mick Doyle, who died so tragically this year. Mick was a great friend of mine. Doyler and his wife Mandy were at my wedding, and it was probably Doyler more than anyone else who encouraged me to become a sports pundit. Mick used to come to Kerry on holidays and bought a house there and we became good friends. Unconsciously I suppose I imitated Doyle's style on the telly, as I have a lot of Doyler's traits in me.

I was at the game in March when Ireland beat Scotland to win the Triple Crown. What I remember most forcefully about the game was listening to *Ireland's Call* before the match. It would not psyche up a person to go into battle. The night before the game, Mick Doyle was asked what it was he most disliked about rugby today. He replied: 'I'm not sure whether it's Brian O'Driscoll's hair or *Ireland's Call*.'

I suppose what I took most from Mick was a desire to marry analysis with entertainment. However, this can be difficult as there are a number of pitfalls facing a television pundit. There are a number of golden rules a pundit should adhere to, the first of which is to be careful what you say – not something I am noted for!

It is also important not to get carried away with yourself on television. I'll never forget the night before the All-Ireland final in 1980, the year Kerry played Roscommon in the final. Jimmy Deenihan was interviewed by telephone from the team hotel by Liam O'Murchu on RTÉ's special *Up for the Match* programme.

Liam asked Jimmy: *'An raibh tú ag féachaint ar an gclár?'*

He replied: *'Ní raibh. Bhíomar ag féachaint ar* Match of the Day.'

Apparently the Roscommon players were watching the programme at the time and got a great laugh from Jimmy's answer. Mind you it was probably the only laugh they got that weekend!

That is not to say that you can't be passionate. There are a number of things about the GAA that make my blood boil and I use my platform as a pundit to draw attention to these issues.

Straight from the Heart

Sadly Rule 42 is not the only blind spot of GAA officialdom in wonderland. There are so many others, it is hard to know where to begin. In recent years, one of their most glaring inadequacies has been shown in the use of video evidence. After the 2003 League final, the Games Administration Committee (GAC) used video evidence to crucify Tyrone's Gavin Devlin. A few months later, though, they refused to use it to clear Kildare's Alan Barry and Down's Gregory McCartan. One of the most redeeming features of the human condition is admitting that you have made a mistake. Unfortunately, those in higher echelons of the GAA are particularly reluctant to admit when they got it wrong, even if the video evidence is conclusive.

The GAA could learn from the way other sports use video evidence. In 2000, 22-year-old Tracy Sargent streaked at an indoor bowls event. One could not help but be impressed by the diligence of the officials and their commitment to the cause of duty. They later issued a statement: 'Having studied the incident on 43 occasions, including slow-motion replays, we have decided against implementing a rule that spectators should remain clothed at all times.'

There are other inconsistencies in the GAA other than that of video evidence. To take one example, Brendan Ger O'Sullivan and Colin Corkery both got sent off in Cork's last game in the 2003 Championship and missed the opening game of this year's Championship as a result. However, Garret Phelan got sent off in Leitrim's last game in the 2003 Championship, yet he was available for Leitrim's opening game against Roscommon this year.

When it comes to disciplinary matters in general, it sometimes seems to me that the GAA's attitude is: see no evil, hear no evil. The 1985 All-Ireland semifinal between Dublin and Mayo is best remembered for the so-called 'John Finn incident' in which the Mayo half-back sustained a broken jaw in an off-the-ball 'challenge'. Despite a protracted investigation, no action was ever taken against a Dublin player. If you look back on the video, it's obvious John was on the other side of the field from the action as he was attacked. Everybody knows who the culprit was, but he got away as free as a bird. It was heroic for John to play on with a broken jaw. He deserved more from the GAA, but despite much tut-tutting and wringing of hands no action was taken against the player in question. Given my history of using the word 'thugs', I am going to reserve judgement, or at least comment, on this particular incident.

Chairman of the Boards

County Boards also have a lot to answer for. In cases where managers are being paid, the exact figures should be revealed. I know, however, that there is a fat chance of this happening. You have a better chance of seeing me beat Kylie Minogue in the competition for 'Rear of the Year' than seeing any action on that front. Lip service rules okay.

In recent years, the GAA's relationship with amateurism has been riddled with hypocrisy. Despite the spate of rumours that have bedevilled the GAA recently about payments to managers, the Association has been powerless to act because of absence of proof. Former President Peter Quinn famously observed that, while there were many claims that managers were being paid under the table, the GAA couldn't even find the tables.

There are three flourishing black markets in the GAA. First, there is the payment of inter-county managers. According to my sources, about half the football managers in the country are being paid, with three getting more than €100,000 a year. Second, there is payment to club managers and trainers. Take the example of Cork, which considers itself to be the great bastion of amateurism. I am told that in the case of football and hurling, the going rate for a junior club is €80 a night, and for a senior club it is €100–120 a night. Third, there is the payment to players to transfer from one club to another in Dublin, or to transfer from those outside Dublin. There are a certain few who aren't being paid to transfer, but there are a lot who are.

I do not have any problem with managers getting adequately remunerated. In most instances inter-county managers are not paid by the County Board, but are funded by Supporters Clubs through a few wealthy backers. It does create a problem, though, if players know their manager is getting paid handsomely when they themselves have turned down opportunities for overtime to go training or to play a match. What I do find particularly galling, though, is that when so many managers are getting large amounts of money at both club and county level, the GAA effectively turn their eyes away, yet they still get worked into a moral frenzy talking about 'the amateur ethos of the organisation'. Just another incidence of the GAA's ostrich syndrome. The whole 'amateur ethos' mantra is another sacred cow.

Although amateurism in rugby apparently ended abruptly, the reality was that the cracks had been there for years, and widened every season. The big question that will invariably threaten the GAA's core philosophy is: Can the amateur ethos be sustained? Gaelic games remain the last bastions of amateurism among the major sports in Ireland. It does not take a prophet to appreciate that the GAA's unique position will come under serious attack in the coming years.

As major sponsorship deals continue to fill the GAA's coffers, the question of pay for play will inevitably present itself with ever-increasing urgency. Innovative approaches will be required to keep players happy, especially as many continue to receive miserly mileage allowances. I would like to see the GAA pursue a more aggressive strategy when it comes to marketing and sponsorship to raise more money for coaching young players.

The GAA have to put its money where its mouth is to ensure that we have a new generation of DJ Careys, Michael Donnellans and Peter Canavans. This will call for a new mindset where the GAA ends its fixation with bricks and mortar. To take an example, Limerick County Board has developed a stadium which holds 50,000 people. It will be filled three times a year and half-filled twice a year. They are massively in debt, or at least they were before they recently got JP McManus' millions. Thomond Park is entirely unsuitable for the large attendances which the Munster rugby team attracts. Surely it makes financial sense for the GAA in Limerick to open their doors to the Munster rugby team? The money raised could then go to promoting Gaelic games in the Limerick region.

I know only too well how problematic sponsorship can be for the GAA. A lot of people will still remember the phrase: 'Only Bendix Could Whitewash This Lot.' This was the slogan that accompanied a full-page advertisement in two Sunday newspapers on the morning of Sunday, 22 September, 1985 – All-Ireland final Sunday. The ad featured Mick O'Dwyer and members of the Kerry team in a state of undress as they posed adjacent to a washing machine. The resulting furore took the spotlight away from the clash between Kerry and Dublin and there were hysterical comments all round.

I know this is going to send the blood pressure of GAA officials through the roof, but I think yet again the GAA can learn from the experience of soccer here. Earlier this year I went to a Premier League match between Arsenal and Charlton. What struck me on attending the game in North London was the huge amount of merchandising on offer for supporters to buy. Every conceivable item bearing the Arsenal game and logo was available. Is it any wonder that soccer players are more identifiable and so popular, given the huge amount of marketing involved in their sport? Contrast that to a National League match, where the GAA have a captive audience of 4,000 adults and kids at each game yet not a single county jersey or souvenir is on sale. So we shouldn't be surprised when Irish kids adopt cross-channel soccer stars as their heroes, simply because the counties and the Association do so little to promote its players and teams.

As a teacher it constantly depresses me that the GAA have very few role models that appeal to youngsters, unlike soccer or rugby. In that context, a friend of mine was telling me that he sent his son to the Roy Keane school of excellence. The boy came back full of petulance, wouldn't sit in the back of the car and refused to share a room! He thought he had it bad until he talked to his neighbour. He had sent his son to the Keith Wood school of excellence. He came back fat and bald!

In fairness the GAA has picked up a few things from the soccer world, especially the way it has sold block seats in the new Croke Park. Mind you, it has taken a while for everyone to figure out that they should get the most out of these seats. I saw that at first hand myself the first year when I noticed that the two seats next to mine had been empty for every match during the year. Puzzled as to why anyone would spend all that money on these tickets and never use them, my confusion deepened when, at the first match of the second year, a middle-aged man and his teenage son occupied the seats. Unable to contain my curiosity any longer, at half-time I turned to the man and asked why he hadn't used the seats until that point in the season. 'They were a Christmas present from the wife,' replied the Longford man with a weary expression, 'and she didn't actually tell us about them until Christmas Day.'

County Boards also annoy me sometimes. They need to devise a proper programme of games to cater for club players and run it on schedule. They also need to explain what they expect of their team managers. Offaly's Paul O'Kelly was dumped last year without explanation after just one season in the job. What was he expected to achieve in that space of time? Last year his team was beaten in the Leinster Championship, but only after a replay. They were beaten subsequently by a point in the Qualifiers. He was unlucky as the Offaly County Board showed him no mercy and he was sacked. One wonders what this group of men want. They appoint Gerry Fahy as manager, he gets them promoted to Division One and they only lose to Westmeath by a point – which wasn't a point at all – in the Leinster Championship, yet in September Fahy was only reappointed by one vote. He subsequently resigned, believing he did not have adequate support from the County Board. Who could blame him in the circumstances? These guys must think Offaly are back in the glory days of 1982. A reality check is badly needed.

The GAA's ability to snatch defeat from the jaws of victory never ceases to amaze me. More than anything else, Gaelic football and, more particularly, hurling need new counties coming through to win honours to breathe new life into the sport. We saw what Clare did for hurling in 1995 and then Wexford the following year. In 2003, the GAA should have been dancing for joy when Laois won the Leinster final. But what did they do? They imposed a fine of €1,400 on the Laois County Board because a Laois defender, Joe Higgins, brought his twin sons, six-year-olds Jack and Kevin, with him during the pre-match parade!

Should we be surprised? Not in the least. When Kerry played Roscommon in the 1980 All-Ireland final there was controversy in the build-up because Dermot Earley had led his four-year-old son David with him during the pre-match parade in the All-Ireland semifinal against Armagh. Few players have made a greater contribution to the game than Dermot Earley in a career that spanned 20 years in the Roscommon colours. Yet instead of honouring him, the GAA went into a tizzy because he had committed that most of heinous of crimes. He had broken a rule. Talk about warped priorities.

Diary of a GAA Analyst
Saturday, 8 May, 2004, saw the first *Sunday Game* meeting of the year. There is a new team in charge, new music, new graphics and games will come live from the venues. The papers are criticising it before it even starts as change for change's sake. A website was started up to force RTÉ to change the theme music. Many thousands of signatures were produced, but it started to lose its credibility when the names included George Bush and Osama Bin Laden. One prominent GAA official got on his high horse and sent in a lot of emails about the programme, but as far as I know RTÉ only got one other letter of complaint and one phone call about it.

There are new panellists like Larry O'Gorman and Anthony Tohill. I got a new role presenting the Sunday night programme for the season, with Michael Lyster presenting the programme live from the venues. Last year I went to two matches. It is difficult to do proper analysis from the studio, because you are relying on what the cameraman is showing you, what the director is showing you, and what the commentator and co-commentator are telling you. Not only do you miss out on the atmosphere, you miss out on the totality of what is happening.

Another new change for *The Sunday Game* is that telestrator is going to be used, the system where you have the Xs and Os. If the soccer boys can do it then so can we. Mind you, we only used it twice!

We have a planning meeting every Sunday at 6.00 pm to discuss what we are going to do on the programme. I have my preparation work done, and I try and predict what we will be the talking points for the first match in the new season, Derry versus Tyrone. I had written down the following: blanket defences, loads of fouling and referee's inconsistencies. What happens in the game? Absolutely nothing. We were stuck for something to say. The game was brutal, devoid of all atmosphere and the referee was consistent. Wonder of wonders there were only 37 frees. That must be a new record for a Derry–Tyrone clash.

In the Carlow–Longford match, with Luke Dempsey having only been appointed Carlow manager three weeks previously, I confidently predicted in my column that it is a bit like rearranging the deckchairs on the *Titanic* and Carlow have no chance. What happens? Carlow create the first big shock of the Championship and beat Longford. In one of his typical media-shy performances, when Luke was interviewed afterwards he said the Carlow players took a few weeks to get used to his 'style of football'. Luke, if you're reading this, let me know what the secret is to your style of football. I promise I won't tell anyone.

My new role is to ask questions. While this is great in one way, the main problem is that when we are discussing football I'm bursting to butt in and give my opinions, but I have to bite my tongue. It is easier in hurling because I'm not as knowledgeable about the clash of the ash. On the plus side, as a 'neutral' interviewer, I hope to wake up the next morning knowing I haven't offended anybody. My first night in the presenter's chair did not go smoothly. The centrepiece of the programme was the coverage of the National League hurling final. In a new departure this year, RTÉ are spending a lot of money sending a camera crew out to the venues. After Galway's victory, Marty Morrissey interviewed Eugene Cloonan, Derek Hardiman and Conor Hayes live from Gort. The three Galway men were very subdued and the small crowd behind them were very muted. Marty ended his piece by saying, 'The party will continue into the small hours.' I had the misfortune to say, 'What party? I have seen livelier wakes.'

It didn't go down well in Galway. Cyril Farrell texted our panellist Tomás Mulcahy to say that the joke had gone down like a lead balloon. The Championship is only a week old and already I have landed myself in trouble. *Plus ça change.*

I obviously made a big impact however, because after two weeks, the *Irish Independent*'s sports editor PJ Cunningham stated: 'I am sorry to say that Pat Spillane as anchorman in that programme just doesn't work.' Yet early in July, PJ had a change of heart and said that I had grown into the job. It takes a big man to publicly admit that he was wrong. Regardless of his initial opinion of me I applaud him for his moral courage.

Bitter experience has taught me, though, that if someone wants to find fault with you they will. It is a bit like the story of the garda sergeant, a total so and so, who was on his last day in the town before he retired from the force. He was a mean and spiteful man and had 'caught' everyone in the town for some offence or other. The only person who had escaped was the parish priest. The garda was determined to rectify that situation on his last day. He knew that the priest always cycled down a hill on his way home after saying morning mass, so the garda stood at the bottom of the hill. His plan had been to step out in front of the priest, forcing him to swerve and topple over, and then he could 'do him' for dangerous driving. He carried out his plan, but although the priest swerved, he kept control of his bike. The priest stopped, though, to wish the garda well on his retirement. The cop said, 'Jesus, you were fierce lucky not to fall then.'

The priest replied, 'Indeed I was lucky, but then I had God with me.'

The garda nearly danced for joy as he said, 'In that case, I'm doing you for having two on a bike.'

When Honesty Is Not the Best Policy

To thine own self be true. It was all very well for Shakespeare to write that but he obviously hadn't a GAA analyst in mind when he got that brainwave. Telling it as it is, in my signature style, has got me into no end of trouble.

If you get a reputation for being an early riser you can stay in bed all day. It's the same idea for a GAA analyst. As soon as I mention referees, people think I am doing a hatchet job. Likewise when people hear me talking about Ulster football, they immediately think of my 'puke football' comment. People remember the sound bite but they forget the context. What people have to realise is that when you are analysing a game, especially a live one, the adrenalin is flowing. In 2002, I described some of Kerry's football against Cork as 'orgasmic'. It is not the sort of comment I would normally make.

This May I got into trouble when Fr Seamus Gardiner, Chairman of the National Referees Committee, criticised me for an interview I did on *The Sunday Game* with Bernard Flynn, regarding the dismissal of Wicklow's Ciaran Clancy against

Meath. A national newspaper carried the headline: 'Refs' chief furious over RTÉ's "diabolical" criticism'. It was suggested that the debate was one-sided and totally biased against the referee. I know damn well that many people in the GAA are all too eager to have a go at me, but what really happened? I was making a general point, which wasn't specifically directed against the referee, that six months training should not go down the drain because of human error. As for balance, I actually defended the referee, pointing out that he had to make a split-second decision without any help from anybody. When Bernard suggested that weaker counties are more sinned against in these cases, I asked him why he held that opinion. Surely a balanced question on my part? I have the utmost respect for referees, and I'm on record as saying that refereeing standards have improved in recent years. But we simply cannot turn a blind eye when mistakes are made. The reality is that we could devote huge chunks of every *Sunday Game* programme to highlighting refereeing errors. It is a sign of maturity on the part of any organisation that it holds its hands up and admits that mistakes are made, and is prepared to do something about them. It would be nice to think this would be the road the GAA would go down, but I am not holding my breath.

At the end of our *Sunday Game* season, we received a nice letter from the Referees Association complimenting us on our fairness to referees throughout the year. I also found it interesting to see details of the Referees Committee at the end of September. It claimed that, of the 57 games they observed, 27 were very good, 27 were good and three were fair. Somehow I think a referee's committee may not be the best judge of a referee's performance!

I personally think that the referee's workload is too high. Apart from having to watch the on-the-ball action, there is the off-the-ball action, keeping the score and keeping the time. They have two linesmen to help them and four umpires and a referee's assistant, whose job is to hold up the board that shows how much time is left. I think the assistant could take some of the load off the referee. This is desirable as the referee's job is getting increasingly difficult, particularly when you consider Joe Brolly's claim that players are deliberately manufacturing fouls to get players sent off and referees are being hoodwinked.

In 2004 it seemed that every second game had a controversy about whether a particular ball had been a point or a wide. To take one example, Westmeath beat Offaly by a point. In the 22nd minute, Westmeath's Brian Morley had been awarded a point for a ball that went wide. Offaly went out of the Leinster Championship. As the stakes are so high, I think there should be video evidence just to cover these circumstances. Mind you, George Hook would make the point that video evidence doesn't guarantee you total accuracy. Most people will remember the surprise when Brian O'Driscoll was awarded a try by the video referee against France in 2001. In the Ulster hurling final between Antrim and Down there was a controversial incident. We froze the ball. It crossed over the top of the upright. So what do you do then?

Some people said that showing live games would be the death knell for the GAA, but in fact the opposite is the case. The GAA still put up plenty of obstacles to RTÉ, however, like preventing games being shown on Saturday evenings at 6 pm. Last year, though, one of the biggest TV audiences ever came in a Saturday evening match between Roscommon and Kildare, which was a great game and a brilliant advertisement for Gaelic football. The GAA want us to show games on Saturday afternoons, but there just isn't the same audience there then. In terms of showcasing your product, it is the difference between having your shop on a side-street or on Grafton Street.

The GAA seem to think that RTÉ should be an extension of the GAA's PR department, but if you want publicity you have to expect it warts and all. For me one of the biggest warts is violent play, but speaking out about this has brought me no end of trouble.

On *The Sunday Game*, after Armagh played Derry in the Ulster Championship in 1996, I infamously used the word 'thugs' to describe what is euphemistically known in the GAA vernacular as 'robust play'. The following Sunday, RTÉ asked me to withdraw the remark but certainly not to apologise. I said I would and agreed to do it off the cuff the next Sunday night. I was doing fine until I said if they had done the same thing outside the ground they would be 'criminals'. So I took one step forward and two miles back!

The next morning I was hauled in front of the Head of Sport in RTÉ, Tim O'Connor. It was one of the scariest moments of my life. There are three times in my life I have felt intimidated. The first was when the Dean of St Brendan's caught me out of the dormitory late at night and reprimanded me. The second was when a tax inspector gave me a grilling about my taxes. The third time was when Tim O'Connor carpeted me. I was in fear because I thought it was the end of the line. To be perfectly honest, it looked like it was curtains for me in RTÉ. Obviously RTÉ Sport were afraid of legal action. They had had problems in the past over what seemed a harmless enough remark. They were panicking a little that they were going to get stung again. In the end they scripted an apology, which I read out from an autocue, and I got away with it. I checked it out with a barrister friend of mine afterwards and asked him if calling someone a 'thug' is libellous. He said yes. It is only okay to call someone a blackguard.

The only other time I got into serious trouble as an analyst came on Saturday, 12 August, 2000. It was the day of the Leinster senior football replay. Dublin led by 0–11 to 0–5 at half-time and had swept aside the Kildare challenge in the second quarter, scoring seven points without reply and playing some thrilling football. Kildare brought on two subs at half-time, two of their 'imports', Karl O'Dwyer and Brian Murphy. I was in jocose mood and said Karl couldn't get on to the Kerry team and Brian wouldn't have got on the Cork Junior team. Within 90 seconds of the re-start, the picture had changed dramatically as Kildare got a two goal blitz and Dublin collapsed and only scored a single point in the second half. Yet again, I was left looking silly and fully expected to eat humble pie, but there was much more in store.

All hell broke loose. To my mind it was completely over the top. I was making just a few tongue-in-cheek observations, as is my wont, and had not intended to be taken too seriously, but it seemed to be the end of the world to people in Kildare. There was a huge sign outside Monasterevin to the effect that Spillane was a goat. I was driving through Kildare for the next few weeks on wet Monday mornings with sunglasses on in case anyone recognised me. It was just ridiculous. The most sinister reaction was apparent when I was shown a letter in RTÉ from one of the most influential GAA officials in Kildare demanding that an apology be issued and that I be dropped as an analyst by RTÉ, otherwise he would ensure that the GAA would not renew their contract with RTÉ. As the contract negotiations were imminent, the powers that be in RTÉ were genuinely very worried about this threat.

When all the vitriol was over, I had survived the sort of sequence that could have broken me, but whose main effect has been to increase my self-sufficiency and strengthen my capacity to live with the fickleness of other people's reactions to my personality. Like studying for the Leaving Cert, it was unpleasant at the time, but retrospectively worth the endurance. Whenever people are giving me a hard time, I always think of Brendan Behan's dictum: 'All publicity is good, except an obituary notice.'

Even when it means I sound as politically correct, in GAA terms, as a Nuremberg rally, I call a spade a spade and not an agricultural implement. Accordingly, to explain the duty of the GAA analyst I think of the parable of the donkey and the bridge.

A man and his son were bringing their donkey to the fair. The man was walking with the donkey and his son was up on the animal's back. A passer-by said, 'Isn't it a disgrace to see that poor man walking and the young fella up on the donkey having an easy time. He should walk and let his poor father have a rest.'

So the boy dismounted and the father took his place. A mile later they met another man who said, 'Isn't it a disgrace to see that man sitting up on the donkey's back and his poor son walking. He should let his son get up on the donkey with him.'

When the man heard this, he instructed his son to get up on the donkey's back with him. After they travelled another mile they met a woman. She said, 'Isn't it a disgrace to see those two heavy men up on that poor little donkey's back. They should get down off him and carry the donkey for a change.'

The father and son dismounted, got a pole from the side of the road and tied the donkey to it and they carried him across their shoulders. Then disaster struck. Tragically as they walked over the bridge the donkey fell into the river and drowned. The moral of the story is that if you are an analyst and you are trying to please everyone you might as well kiss your ass goodbye.

The Price of Fame

Gaelic football is drama's first cousin. It is theatre without the script. So I know I am very lucky to have this wonderful job. But it is not as glamorous or as lucrative as people think.

A lot of people asked me whether Colm O'Rourke and I got a pay rise when we briefly went on strike last year. Sadly not. We won't be giving up the day job. The only interesting thing to emerge was that we discovered that the vast percentage of the budget for analysts in RTÉ Sport apparently goes to a few other gentlemen in another sport who shall remain nameless. We discovered that the GAA analysts are not exactly at the top of the scale when it comes to pay. Our critics would probably say we did not deserve a pay rise in the first place, especially those who persist in comparing us to Statler and Waldorf, the two old men from *The Muppet Show*.

When you present a high-profile programme on national television you are not nearly as pampered as I expected. On my first day in the job, when meal time came, I went to the RTÉ canteen for lunch. 'What are my choices?' I asked. The man behind the counter replied, 'Yes or no.'

The biggest change is that I get recognised way more now than I ever did as a player. After any of the All-Irelands I played in, when I walked down Grafton Street only one or two people recognised me. Now a lot of people recognise me. They may not all know my name but they know my face. Sometimes I am asked: 'Are you the fella on the television?' Less flattering is: 'Are you somebody?' The most sickening was: 'Didn't you used to be Pat Spillane?'

I am reminded of the day Lester Piggott went into a shop to buy an ice-cream. The excited girl at the counter asked, 'Are you Wilson Pickett?'

There is an amusing website that has a diary of a Kerry football pundit. According to this, the only reason why I spend any time in RTÉ is to try and catch the eye of Sharon Ní Bheolain. That's so untrue. Those of us fortunate enough to work in RTÉ Sport have no need to be drooling over Sharon. We have our very own sex symbol – Marty Morrissey!

The Last Word

How do I sum up my life as analyst? I can only quote the wise words of David Brent, star of *The Office*: 'Accept that some days you are the pigeon, and some days you are the statue.'

What does posterity need me for? Nothing. But what would I like said about me at my funeral? I'd like someone to say, 'Look! He's moving!'